W9-CTK-280

In Shackleton's Wake

In Shackleton's Wake

ARVED FUCHS

Translated by
Martin Sokolinsky

S

Sheridan House

First published 2001
In the United States of America by
Sheridan House, Inc.
145 Palisade Street
Dobbs Ferry, NY 10522
www.sheridanhouse.com

First published in Germany under the title
Im Schatten des Pols
by Verlag Delius, Klasing & Co. KG. Bielefeld

Library of Congress Cataloging-in-Publication Data

Fuchs, Arved
    [Im Schatten des Pols. English]
    In Shackleton's wake/Arved Fuchs;
    Translated by Martin Sokolinsky.
        p.cm
    Includes bibliographical references (p.)
    ISBN 1-57409-138-7 (alk. paper)
      1. Fuchs, Arved—Journeys—Antarctica.
      2. Shackleton, Ernest Henry, Sir, 1874-1922—
Journeys—Antarctica.
      3. Antarctica—Description and travel. I. Title

    G850 2000. F83 F8413 2001
    919.8'904—dc21   2001034839

Edited by Janine Simon
Designed by Jesse Sanchez

Printed in the United States of America

ISBN   1-57409-138-7

For Brigitte

Contents

In Shackleton's Wake

Prologue

Our breath emerged from under our facemasks in thick clouds. Some of the moisture formed ice crystals that settled on our beards and hoods. As the hours dragged by, the lower half of my face was covered by a thick coat of ice; the upper half was framed by my dark goggles and the fur-rimmed hood of my parka.

Like an automaton, deep in thought, I shoved one ski ahead of the other. The skis crunched over crystal ice that gale-force winds and the cold had polished. The irregular jolts on the harness of the sled I was towing yanked me out of my reverie.

After 48 days, the sled had finally become noticeably lighter. Day after day, I had dragged its original 260-pound weight from sea level up to an altitude of 8,400 feet. Over frozen-channeled drifts, across yawning glacial crevasses, against winds often attaining gale force, the cold grew even more biting and the sled acted like a drogue parachute. Retreat into a world of my own brought relief. In my mind's eye, I saw the faces of close friends; I saw lush gardens whose flowers I thought I could smell. In my imagination I talked to people and made plans for my future. But every now and then I tore myself away from these fantasies and, through polarized goggles, studied a landscape almost unchanged since the start of our expedition.

The trail was hard and uneven. The tracks of our skis on the windswept ground were hardly visible, and even the heavy sleds left their furrows only at odd intervals—whenever a runner broke through the icy snow drifts. The wasteland we were crossing could not have been more inhospitable: It was the height of the summer season; yet it was cold, barren and bleak, without the slightest sign of life. There was not so much as a bird, a small animal or even a patch of moss or lichens. No place on earth could be so desolate. Just the two of us, Reinhold Messner and I, with our sleds that carried everything we needed for survival in this Antarctic desert. Without these supplies, we were lost. Their presence was a stark reminder of our own frailty, for we simply didn't belong here; this was truly no-man's land.

In the previous twelve months I had seen a great deal of snow and ice; I had experienced a great deal of cold, perhaps too much. By the time this trip was over I would have covered, including mileage done in training, about 2,000 miles on skis under extreme conditions. And in so doing, I would become the first man to reach the North and South Poles on foot within a single year. For me, this was really a journey from Pole to Pole that had begun months earlier on the ice-bound coast of Northern Canada.

Now I was en route to the South Pole.

Despite all the hardships, an experienced polar traveler can withstand the cold of the Antarctic summer. Except for the crevassed tongues of glaciers, the technical problems of the terrain are relatively insignificant. Antarctica's immensity is the real issue. Men on foot simply cannot comprehend the distances that must be covered to reach their goal. Distance and the time factor are the real dangers; again and again, these are underestimated. Antarctica is totally unforgiving. Inexperienced travelers who lose their way quickly run out of supplies and energy. Then it is only a matter of hours until the icy wasteland stifles all life, as Scott and his men found to their cost.

Each morning you pull yourself out of your sleeping bag instead of simply continuing to lie there. Each morning you motivate yourself all over again and keep yourself from wondering, "Why on earth am I doing this to myself?" all the while knowing that a freezing eight- or nine-hour slog lies ahead and that it will end that evening with the sobering realization that the miles so painfully covered can hardly be picked out on the chart because its scale is far too large for the day's pitiful distance. After a very long time those tiny dots on the chart finally add up and yield the desired distance. But it will take days, weeks, months!

The Antarctic traveler turns inwards, building a protective wall out of dreams and plans for the future. This mental shield is a protection from the overwhelming power of nature. But, mercifully, there are also days when the sun shines, there is no wind, and I can take in this untouched natural landscape and be moved by its grandeur. This is the moment to breathe deeply, to regain my composure, to prepare for the next onslaught.

The North and South Poles are quite literally the ends of the earth. Nowhere else is the cold on our planet felt so acutely. Both, more so than any other natural landscape, best symbolize the daring and endurance of individual explorers, as well as of entire nations, during the great age of discovery.

Antarctica is a vast landmass where life only exists in the coastal zones. In the Arctic—and even at the North Pole—one finds seals, Arctic foxes, polar bears or sea birds. The interior of Antarctica, by contrast, is a barren, storm-bound wasteland. It is the coldest place on earth. Explorers in East Antarctica have taken readings of minus 89.7 degrees Celsius—the coldest temperatures ever recorded on the planet.

I was prepared for it, as I harnessed myself to my heavy sled and took the first step in the direction of the South Pole; I still felt prepared when, 48 days later, against wind and hail, I trekked the last mile to my objective.

After another 1,000 miles, in part by a route never before used, and after a total of 92 days on the ice, Reinhold Messner and I reached the other side of the Antarctic continent. We were exhausted, filthy, and obsessed with a desire to escape to the warmth and comfort of civilization. But other than a few sprains and minor cuts, we arrived intact. We had done something hitherto considered impossible by many experts; we had crossed Antarctica on foot.

To a degree, the task we had taken on, and now accomplished, had a historical dimension. No less a figure than Sir Ernest Shackleton, the British explorer, had laid the cornerstone for this crossing. When he sailed from England in ENDURANCE in 1914, he had in mind just such a crossing, the one that, 75 years later, we would finally make. If we disregard the so-called "Commonwealth Expedition" which, in the

1950s, crossed the continent in airplanes and tracked vehicles, no one had ever traversed the Antarctic on foot. We were the first.

Shackleton's "Imperial Trans-Antarctic Expedition" had failed from the start. Despite warnings about unusually severe ice conditions, ENDURANCE left South Georgia and sailed into the ice-choked Weddell Sea. She would never leave the ice. For Shackleton's men, the odyssey on the pack ice was to become a race for life.

In her first winter, beset by the ice, the ship drifted a long way from the coast. In the end, despite her massive construction, she succumbed to the encroaching ice and broke up. As the sinking took some time, the men were able to recover sufficient quantities of gear and provisions. But to what end? There could be no place more desolate for a shipwreck than the Weddell Sea. For months they drifted slowly with the ice. Significantly, they named their last camp "Patience Camp," a virtue that would be continuously demanded of them. Finally, after months of drifting, their ice floe reached open water. Shackleton gave the order to launch the three lifeboats salvaged from the ENDURANCE, thus starting their own rescue voyage. And that is precisely where my story begins.

The rescue journey began in three small open boats that made their way through the ice fields of the Weddell Sea to barren, uninhabited Elephant Island. There, Shackleton left behind 22 men and two of the boats. He selected five men and set out in the sturdy JAMES CAIRD for lonely South Georgia—over 700 nautical miles away. This meant braving the world's stormiest ocean in a 22-foot lifeboat with a six-foot beam. When, by sheer miracle, they reached the island, they had to cross a range of ice-covered mountains to get help from the whaling station on the other side. Somehow, these men climbed South Georgia's uncharted glacial backbone that is often swept by the katabatic winds of the Antarctic, winds of 100 knots or more. Gaunt, exhausted, they reached the Stromness whaling station where a rescue effort was organized for the men left behind. All were saved.

It is only after experiencing the incredible conditions in this part of the world that the achievement of Shackleton and his men can be truly appreciated. The tiny boat picking its way through fields of pack ice, castaways left on the narrow strip of gravel beach at Elephant Island, the unprecedented boat journey in the JAMES CAIRD to South Georgia and, finally, the crossing of the island's ice-covered mountains on foot—it boggles the mind. If a novelist had dreamed up this scenario, those familiar with the climatic conditions in this region would laugh it off as cheap fiction. But the story is true.

As I trekked, day after day, over Antarctica's rough face with skis and sled, my thoughts continued to return to the spiritual father of our expedition—Shackleton. It soon became clear to me that, compared to his rescue voyage, our crossing would seem as tame as a Sunday afternoon outing.

Certainly, our 92-day trek across Antarctica demanded strong will, something that did not allow for despair. But our daily progress was largely routine and the monotony of it turned into one of our greatest problems.

As we came to the end of our expedition, we bragged to each other that we had carried out Shackleton's plan for the Imperial Trans-Antarctic Expedition. But that was only half true. We'd landed on Antarctica in a plane coming from Punta Arenas and that had given us a decided advantage over Shackleton. Despite all the hardships we had faced, this advantage threw a different light on our project. By flying in, we skipped the most difficult phase of the overall expedition—namely, the sea voyage to Antarctica. And that was precisely where Shackleton failed.

Since childhood, I have been a seafarer. I learned to swim in the North Sea, and later made the most foolhardy trips by sea kayak—the sea has always held a magical attraction for me. In mid-winter, I rounded Cape Horn in a collapsible, reached the magnetic North Pole by kayak, and paddled another one around the stormy Aleutians. But thinking about Shackleton's exploits always sent shivers down my spine. I kept wondering whether a re-enactment of this rescue operation would be possible.

At the same time I continued to reject the idea strenuously. Setting goals on expeditions always means walking a tightrope. One step too far and you take a nasty fall. As I am rather attached to life, I make it a matter of policy to set goals that either allow for success or permit a safe and orderly retreat. I shun self-destructive elements. I have never believed in success at any price. Nevertheless, I remained fascinated with Shackleton's journey and could never quite stop wondering about it.

Then the unexpected happened. In 1997, the "Arctic-Antarctic" exhibition opened with great fanfare in Bonn. Having contributed to the exhibits, I was standing among other guests, drinking champagne and listening to the opening speeches. I'd hardly had time to look at the other exhibits at the show.

But when the ranks of the guests on opening night began to thin out, I took a look around—and came to an abrupt halt. Right in the middle of the exhibition stood a small white boat, simple and without much equipment. I judged her to be about 21 feet long. She was made completely of wood, her deck canvassed with sailcloth. On the bow her name was written in small black lettering, JAMES CAIRD.

I had never dreamed that the original boat still existed. I had assumed that, since 1916, no one had ever gone to the trouble of bringing this boat—hardly more than a wreck—back from South Georgia. But the JAMES CAIRD now belonged to Dulwich College in London. Shackleton himself had donated the boat to his alma mater.

It took me a while to take it all in. Astonished and somewhat awed, I stood in front of the boat. She looked even smaller and more fragile than I had imagined. And then, suddenly, I was trekking across Antarctica's inland ice again; those old thoughts were back. As I grasped the boat's gunwale with both hands, something just went click in my mind. Without knowing exactly how and why, from that moment I became certain that I was going to re-live Shackleton's journey; I still didn't know exactly how, when or with whom. What made me take that decision was the realization that, over the years, so many experiences had prepared me for this project.

I was not only fascinated by Shackleton's rescue mission but by Ernest Shackleton, the man. Almost affectionately, his men called him the "Boss." And even if his expeditions never attained their goals, this in no way diminished his popularity or his reputation. On the contrary, Shackleton became known for "achieving the impossible." He brought a hitherto unknown human dimension to polar exploration differing basically, in that respect, with his contemporaries Scott, Amundsen or Peary. For him, it was more important to bring all his men home safely than to blindly pursue some goal. Sir Raymond Priestley hit the nail on the head when he said: "For scientific leadership give me Scott; for swift and efficient travel Amundsen; but when there seems no way out, get down on your knees and pray for Shackleton."

Re-enacting his expedition, I would come as close to him as is humanly possible. Only in this way could I understand his thought processes. Literally, I decided to take the plunge. On the return trip from Bonn to Bad Bramstedt, I was deep in thought. I knew that I was facing the most difficult challenge of my career. If I had suspected just how difficult, I would never have started.

1

The Boss

When I began planning the re-enactment of the boat journey after finding the JAMES CAIRD at the exhibition in Bonn, not too many people knew the name Shackleton. A few may have known something about Amundsen, Scott and, perhaps, Peary and Nansen, but the general public had only hazy notions about Shackleton. This situation changed dramatically when the *National Geographic* and *Geo* printed the story of the ENDURANCE in 1998, followed almost immediately by Caroline Alexander's book.

They all featured the retouched, repaired photos taken by Frank Hurley, the photographer for the expedition. Hurley, the man called the "warrior with a camera," the man who "would go any place, any time to get a picture," was not only an inspired photographer and cameraman—he would face any danger or punishment to achieve his goals. Hurley's film *South* about the ENDURANCE is one of the most noteworthy cinematic documents of those times on the exploration of the polar caps. Only Herbert Ponting, a British member of Scott's expedition, could be compared with him. Hurley was a Shackleton man. Perhaps his photos were the decisive factor in this resurgence of interest.

There was no big anniversary, no event of topical interest to catapult Shackleton into the public eye, but suddenly, he was back. Until recently regularly featured only in specialized magazines on explorations and adventures, he became overnight the guru of personnel managers, being praised for his leadership ability and the crisis management skills they imagined in him. The ENDURANCE and Shackleton were suddenly in vogue. I least of all could understand why this happened. Not that I disputed the qualities attributed to him. On the contrary, his crisis management ability fascinated me but, because of my own polar experience, I evaluated his skills in a very specific way and with far less reverence.

I have enormous respect for Shackleton's achievement but, at the same time I am astonished by his lack of planning which in some cases borders on negligence. For me, Shackleton was no icon to be approached with utmost reverence. I had gone through too much in the north and south polar regions for that. What made him interesting were the contradictions inherent in his character. I saw him as a distant colleague with amazing abilities but, also, with flaws and personal problems. Shackleton was just a man and that fact brought him closer to me. I approached him without all this adulation, but also without the criticism of people who really have no understanding of the subject. Without being presumptuous, after more than 20 years of polar exploration, I felt much closer to him than all those who, having fallen in love with a polar traveler of earlier times, now thought they could do a psychological profile of him.

Thus, the plans for my voyage did not originate with the Shackleton craze that sprang up suddenly but, rather, from a gradually maturing interest in this individual who belonged to a dying breed of adventurers and polar explorers.

While ENDURANCE picked her way vainly through the ice fields of the Weddell Sea, the rest of the world was in flames. In the trenches along the Flanders fields and at Verdun, men massacred each other in a bitter conflict. For the first time, poison gas was being used and the war machine soon had motorized vehicles and aircraft pouring off assembly lines. Biplanes engaged in dogfights in the skies over Europe, huge battleships sent projectiles weighing a thousand pounds at targets miles away and the first tanks, spitting death and destruction, clattered over trackless muddy battlefields. But at the same time, polar expeditions were still being made in sailing ships from the previous century. In terms of conquering Terra Incognita, the use of technology had barely changed from the nineteenth century. In 1848 the ships ERE-BUS and TERROR (of the ill-fated John Franklin expedition, which in vain had tried to discover the Northwest Passage in the Arctic) had used steam engines. Thus, Shackleton was the last representative of what has been termed the heroic age of discovery.

He was born in Ireland of an Irish mother and an English father. In his youth Shackleton was drawn to the sea. On April 19, 1890, the sixteen-year-old signed aboard the three-masted square rigger HOUGHTON TOWER and made his first Cape Horn passage. In the middle of a southern winter, the place lived up to its awful reputation: For two months, the windjammer fought gale after gale, finally reaching Valparaiso in mid-August. Then, when the HOUGHTON TOWER headed home for Liverpool in 1891, there were hardly any provisions on board; the fresh water supply ran out. Despite the harsh conditions, Shackleton's passion for the sea did not diminish. Even during the gale-tossed rounding of the Horn, his mind was on the *Terra Australis Incognita*, Antarctica: "I felt strangely drawn by the mysterious South. We rounded the Horn in mid-winter. The whole time an uninterrupted blizzard raged. But even in the face of adversity my thoughts wandered southward," he said in an interview a few years later.

By age twenty, he had gone round Cape Horn no fewer than five times and at 24 earned his master's license on a round-the-world voyage. On September 13, 1900, he volunteered for the National Antarctic Expedition, which Robert Falcon Scott had planned. But Shackleton was rejected. He finally managed to get the appointment through the assistance of one of the sponsors and the president of the Royal Geographical Society.

The only thing that Scott and Shackleton had in common was the desire to be first to reach the South Pole. Scott was a Royal Navy Officer; Shackleton, a captain in the Merchant Marine. They differed basically in their manner of dealing with subordinates, in their personal leadership style. For both men, 1901 was their first voyage to Antarctica. The expedition ship DISCOVERY reached McMurdo Sound where Scott had the men build a hut on land to serve as a base camp.

Scott and Shackleton did not get along. Navy man Scott could not get a handle on Shackleton, the unconventional, charismatic civilian. Shackleton came down with scurvy and, at times, had to be hauled on one of the sleds. The expedition proved anything but successful. The party under Scott reached only 82 degrees 17 seconds south and, thus, never traversed the shelf ice. After returning to the base camp, Scott sent the ailing Shackleton back to Europe—against the man's express wish. This Shackleton took as a humiliation, one for which he never forgave Scott. The two men broke with each other and would henceforth go their respective ways, each keeping a wary eye on the other's activities.

In 1908 Shackleton set out on a South Pole expedition of his own. Its official name was "British Antarctic Expedition," but it was better known by the name of the expedition ship, NIMROD. Shackleton committed planning errors similar to Scott's. Instead of perfecting the technique of cross-country skiing and employing Eskimo dog sleds—well-known for their efficiency—he shipped ponies complete with their stalls and fodder to Antarctica. The poor beasts died one after another on the way to the Pole, so that the expedition had to switch to "man-hauling"—that is, the men pulled the sleds themselves. Just how effective ski and dog sleds could be on this terrain was demonstrated a few years later by the Norwegian Roald Amundsen. Nevertheless, Shackleton and his three companions man-hauled to 88 degrees 23 minutes south, coming within 97 nautical miles of the South Pole. They beat Scott's "furthest south" by a full 366 miles, or 678 kilometers. In so doing, the "highway" to the Pole over the hitherto unknown Beardmore Glacier had been found.

Shackleton decided to turn back when they were only a few days' march from the South Pole, demonstrating his foresight and sense of responsibility to himself and his men. Had he pushed on, had he made it to the Pole—he would certainly have perished on the return journey, just as Scott was to do a few years later. Knowing that the goal—and his place in the history books—was so near and still to turn back shows that, despite all his ambition, Shackleton was guided by serious reflection. Exhausted and starved, he made it back to the coast and to the NIMROD just in time. The return trek became a race with death. Two of his men being too weak to stand the pace, Shackleton and his companion Frank Wild hurried on ahead to stop the ship that was about to sail.

Considering his state of malnutrition, this was an incredible feat. En route, he even gave one of his carefully rationed biscuits to Wild: "Shackleton compelled me to eat one of his only breakfast biscuits and tonight would have given me one more of them had I permitted him to do so. I doubt that anyone in the world can understand the generosity and sympathy that was thereby bestowed on me. I DO—and by God—I shall never forget him for it! No money in the world could have bought that biscuit!"

Shackleton's leadership style, his endurance and his well-known solicitude for his men made him a legend. While he and his three companions were en route to the Pole, he climbed a further section of the 4000-meter Mount Erebus; facing unbelievable danger and hardships, another party reached the magnetic Pole. All in all, it was a highly successful expedition: the first ascent of Mount Erebus, attaining the magnetic South Pole for the first time and almost reaching the geographic South Pole. He had paved the way for its subsequent exploration and had collected a wealth of scientific data. Shackleton had put his archrival Scott in his place and was knighted upon his return. Henceforth, he would be "Sir Ernest."

For all the acclaim, he nevertheless still owed huge bills for the expedition. His debts kept him in England for the next few years. Books and speaking engagements brought in money, but took time. Meanwhile, amid great fanfare, Scott was preparing his second Antarctic Expedition. How Shackleton must have gnashed his teeth watching Scott exploit the "road sign to the Pole" that he, Shackleton, had discovered.

But Scott had a powerful competitor in Roald Amundsen, the Norwegian explorer. While Amundsen's team was composed of skilled skiers and dog-sled drivers, with a total of fifty dogs, Scott repeated the error of the DISCOVERY expedition and, as well, that of Shackleton. Like the latter, Scott gambled on Siberian ponies as a means of transport—and would also meet disaster with them. The skiing was rudimentary—on par with the DISCOVERY expedition.

As for tailoring nutritional plans, little, if anything, had been learned. True, both expeditions had, in theory, allowed approximately 4500 calories per person, per day. But calorific value alone says little about the components of food. Amundsen attached great importance to proper diet and therefore brought food rich in vitamins by the standards of those times. Significantly, the British man-hauling technique meant burning much more energy than dog-sledding where the animals did the bulk of the work. In addition, Amundsen would cover the trail faster, thus keeping the risk of Vitamin C deficiency to a minimum (the body can go without Vitamin C for no more than three months). Amundsen and his team had regained their base camp where there was ample food well before the three months. Meanwhile, in the same timespan, Scott had yet to cover half the route. The outcome is known to all: Scott and his companions met their deaths from exhaustion only ten miles from the depot of food and fuel.

An unparalleled epic, the end of Scott's party became a national tragedy, one that on closer examination might have been avoided. But there was no room for such considerations; Scott's glorious miscalculations were swept under the rug. The waves of emotion ran so high that, for a time, the successful Amundsen was even blamed for Scott's death. Found after his death, Scott's diary showed that he and his men had nourished the myth of endurance and perseverance—right up to their self-destruction. Scott's valiant failure brought him more recognition posthumously than Amundsen who had made almost no mistakes.

All of Britain felt the defeat that the Norwegian had again handed them. For centuries, Englishmen had sought to find the Northwest Passage—sometimes, at great sacrifice. They had failed, but Roald Amundsen did it with his little ship GJöA on the first try. Either Cook or Peary had reached the North Pole (a dispute arose over which American had arrived first), and now the South Pole was being "taken away" from the British by Amundsen.

What was left for men of Shackleton's breed? There seemed to be no goal left that could rival the drama of the South Pole in the mind of the public. Shackleton had to think up something extraordinary if he hoped to find support for a new Antarctic expedition. True to form, Shackleton rose to the occasion.

2

The Imperial Trans-Antarctic Expedition

Men wanted for hazardous journey. Small wages, bitter cold, long months of complete boredom, constant danger, safe return doubtful. Honor and recognition in case of success.

This was the advertisement Sir Ernest Shackleton ran in the *London Times* for his latest undertaking. But just exactly what did he have in mind?

Both the North and the South Poles had been reached. A new Antarctic expedition needed to set a goal that would even outdo the race for the Pole in the public esteem; otherwise, it would hardly be possible to raise the funds necessary for such a project. Shackleton knew this. The Scott trauma had been felt deeply by the whole British nation; the people were not ready to go into a new venture. That is precisely where Shackleton came in. He turned Britain's wounded pride into his asset, not even bothering to cite scientific goals as a pretext for the new expedition. Rather, he set his sights on a goal which, if attained, could restore national pride in the field of polar exploration. He therefore said: "It will be a greater journey than the journey to the Pole and back, and I feel that it is up to the British nation to accomplish this, for we have been beaten at the conquest of the North Pole and beaten at the first conquest of the South Pole. There now remains the largest and most striking of all journeys—the crossing of the Continent."

The message struck home. True, there was also criticism and the legitimate concern that a tragedy like Scott's might be repeated. Finally, however, Shackleton succeeded. The plan called for sailing to Antarctica in two ships. One was to head for McMurdo Sound in the Ross Sea, the region from which all previous attempts at the South Pole had been made. That was the charted area. This party's mission called for setting up caches of food and fuel as close as possible to the Pole.

The other vessel with the main party and Shackleton himself would sail into the Weddell Sea in order to land in the Vahsel Bay area. There, using dog-sleds (he had learned his lesson), they would set out on a new, hitherto untried route to the South Pole. As the plan provided that, on their way back from the Pole, they would find the caches set up by the Ross Sea party, they needed only carry enough provisions and fuel for the way to the Pole and something beyond that. It was an extremely audacious plan, even by the standards of that day.

A major problem for the whole undertaking was the complete lack of communications. As soon as the two parties left the harbor, they were cut off from the outside world. Shackleton had a Morse receiver, but it could be not used for sending. This set, regarded with suspicion by all, was to prove useless. Even if Shackleton and his men had reached the Antarctic continent as planned and arrived at the designated route to the South Pole, they would have to expect the first cache about 500 miles beyond the Pole—assuming that it had actually been set up there at all. At no time could they have been sure that the crew of the AURORA had actually managed to lay down the first supply depot. A thousand things might have happened to the Ross Sea party. Even if the route to the Pole was now charted, it did not banish the memory of another South Pole expedition, one on which Scott and his men had perished. Thus, the failure of this party was at least possible if not actually probable. In addition, the party lacked a genuine polar expert.

Without food depots, the party that started from the Weddell Sea had no chance of reaching the Ross Sea alive. But Shackleton simply dismissed these misgivings. He refused to be surrounded by waverers and doubters. Since he felt so confident about his own plans and there was something vaguely romantic about the goal, he radiated a self-assurance that silenced even the worst skeptics. He knew how to convey the certainty that his planned expedition could be carried out.

Next, obtaining the necessary financial backing represented the biggest stumbling-block. Two ice-worthy vessels had to be acquired, something that meant an enormous sum of money. The largest individual contribution came from the Scottish jute manufacturer Sir James Caird. Alone, he gave $120,000. Shackleton named the largest of the lifeboats after him. Smaller sums were given by Janet Stancomb-Wills as well as Dudley Docker. Their names were inscribed on the ENDURANCE's two other lifeboats.

He received $50,000 from the British government; smaller sums came from the Royal Geographical Society as well as from banks that granted him a loan. As with the NIM-ROD expedition, Shackleton hoped to pay off expenses after the journey with books and lectures. And, it might be added, this procedure for defraying the costs of expeditions has changed very little over the years.

For the Ross Sea party, he purchased the AURORA from Australian explorer Sir Douglas Mawson. Mawson and Shackleton knew each other well from the NIMROD expedition in which Mawson had participated. In the interim he had carried out spectacular expeditions with a more scientific background.

The AURORA had already been used on two Antarctic expeditions. Originally designed as a seal-hunting vessel, she was a stable, ice-worthy ship. The leader of the Ross Sea party was Lieutenant Aeneas Mackintosh, another old comrade from the NIMROD.

For the second ship, Shackleton bought the POLARIS in Norway. One hundred and forty-five feet (48 meters) long, she had a beam of 25 feet (8 meters). Only eighteen months old, she still lay in the shipyard, as the owners had run out of money for completing her. Bought for $67,000, the ship's market value was considerably higher. Shackleton, with a snap decision, had gotten a vessel that was extremely sea-worthy and practically new. He changed the ship's name to ENDURANCE and brought her back to England. The vessel was incredibly strong and built of only select materials.

According to Alfred Lansing, "Her keel members were four pieces of solid oak, one above the other, adding up to a total thickness of 7 feet, 1 inch. Her sides were made from oak and Norwegian mountain fir, and they varied in thickness from about 18 inches to more than 2½ feet. Outside this planking, to keep her from being chafed by the ice, there was a sheathing from stem to stern of greenheart, a wood so heavy it weighs more than solid iron and so tough that it cannot be worked with ordinary tools. Her frames were not only double-thick, ranging from 9¼ to 11 inches, but they were double in number, compared with a conventional vessel." Likewise, her stem was unusually solid. Made of laminated select oak timbers, the stem had a total thickness of 4½ feet (1.30 meters) and thus could withstand the impact of severe collisions with the ice.

Shipbuilding know-how was what made ENDURANCE such a unique vessel, not just the dimensions of the individual components. The men working at the Framnaes Shipyard in Norway were the best in their field and offered a lifetime of experience in the building of sealers and whalers meant for ice conditions. These men understood pack ice and knew precisely what counted in the construction of a ship.

Actually, the builders were working on their dream-ship: when the keel was laid, enough funding had been available to allow them to build her exactly as they would for themselves. Thus, ingenious bracing was placed below decks to give the hull the needed rigidity and integrity under the anticipated pressure of the ice. All fastenings, the treenails, the workmanship as a whole were the best that the shipbuilding trade had to offer at the time. If there was one country that understood how to build ships for voyages through ice, it was Norway.

No ship in the world could match ENDURANCE with the exception of the FRAM, built by Colin Archer for Fridtjof Nansen and used by Amundsen on the South Pole expedition. FRAM, with her egg-shaped hull, had been built without compromise, exclusively for survival in the ice. She therefore had poor sea-going qualities; on the other hand, ENDURANCE sailed well.

Where a journey has its own requirements, no compromise can be permitted. ENDURANCE was designed for hunting seals and polar bears in the loose ice of the polar sea—FRAM for drifting in pack ice. The loss of the extraordinary ENDURANCE resulted simply from using her for the wrong purpose.

As for her rig, ENDURANCE was a three-masted topsail schooner. She was equipped with a 350-horsepower steam engine that gave her a speed of 10 knots plus maneuverability in the ice. No one anticipated that this vessel would be destroyed in pack ice—least of all, her own builders.

The captain of the ENDURANCE was Frank Worsley, a New Zealander who, like Shackleton, had been going to sea since the age of sixteen. For Shackleton, the sea voyages were simply the means to an end—to get from England to Antarctica—but Worsley lived for sailing. Even after the expedition, he would time and again assume exciting commands. In taking these assignments, nothing mattered to him as much as keeping away from the steam-powered vessels with auxiliary sails that had come into vogue. Worsley was a dyed-in-the-wool sailor—and a first-class navigator. Shackleton always spoke to the Skipper in a friendly, respectful manner. In the course of the expedition, Worsley's seamanship would play a key role.

On August 1, 1914, ENDURANCE slipped her moorings. Already, the world situation had cast a pall over the expedition. Only days before her sailing, Austria-Hungary had declared war on Serbia and, shortly thereafter, Germany on France. It was only a matter of days until England would declare war on Germany signaling the start of the First World War. Shackleton and his men were deeply affected. As one man, they unhesitatingly offered to place themselves and the ship at the disposal of the Admiralty. But the government—and Winston Churchill, in particular—decided that the expedition would start as planned. The "Imperial Trans-Antarctic Expedition"—better known as the ENDURANCE Expedition—was on its way.

On November 5, 1914, ENDURANCE arrived in the bay of Grytviken, the Norwegian whaling station on South Georgia. At the time, no one knew more about ice and weather conditions in this region of the world than the whalers. Year in and year out, aboard tiny vessels with decks and rigging dangerously ice-coated, they braved storms, ice fields, and fog. Whaling was an incredibly difficult and brutal calling, but it produced seamen of the highest caliber. Anxiously, perhaps skeptically, they watched the expedition that, with its lofty goals, the ENDURANCE had brought to their domain.

Before Amundsen made his crossing of the Northwest Passage in GJÖA in 1903, he made a point of consulting the whalers; they not only set up depots for him but, with advice and recommendations, put him on the way to success. Their help in no way diminished Amundsen's achievement. Rather, it was because he had been so circumspect that he succeeded.

Shackleton also consulted the whalers and, in long conversations, obtained a picture of the ice conditions prevailing in the Weddell Sea. According to these men, the state of the ice that year was worse than ever before. On one visit to the Stromness whaling station, Shackleton met with the Norwegian station manager, Thoralf Sørlle. He and the other whaling captains outlined the climatic conditions for Shackleton.

Basically the Weddell Sea is a gigantic bay holding fields of pack ice all year round. These fields are only broken by isolated areas of water similar to canals that run through the pack. The ice mass moves in a maelstrom, clockwise, creating enormous pressure wherever an obstacle stands in its way. These ice build-ups are significant and therefore dangerous— especially in the western part, in the area of the Antarctic Peninsula. That was also the reason why Shackleton was trying as much as possible to swing to the east; there, the ice could be traversed most readily, as they could sail in the lee of the coast. In his time, James Weddell had also picked this route as early as 1823. Seal hunter and former Royal Navy commander, for whom this body of water is named, Weddell ventured further than anyone before him. With his two ships, JANE and BEAU FOY—sailing vessels without steam—he reached 74 degrees 15 minutes South latitude. In so doing, he went 185 nautical miles further south than the legendary James Cook or any other contemporary. Weddell was only a two-day sail from the Filchner Ice Shelf when he turned back, but he could not have known this. His record stood a long time, as this coast was not explored until the beginning of the 20th century.

On the morning of December 5, 1914, the ENDURANCE weighed anchor and left South Georgia, bound for Antarctica. Two days later, on December 7, they encountered the first pack ice—much further north than usual. By December 24, they had already fallen behind schedule. Despite the difficult ice conditions, they kept managing to find leads in the ice and, at times, things almost seemed to be going Shackleton's way. On January 10, they sighted land which Shackleton named "Cairdland," after his sponsor, James Caird. Although they were making good headway at this point, their luck would not hold. On January 16, they ran into the edge of nearly impenetrable pack ice. The weather was stormy and the shifting ice pushed the vessel around, jolting her. Under steam she worked her way a little further south but, after another few days, was finally beset. As the weather cleared on January 24 and the visibility improved, they had to acknowledge that the ice had closed in on them. As far as the horizon no open water could be seen—they had fallen in the trap. All efforts to free the ship failed. The almost pathetic attempt to cut a channel through the ice with saws served only to keep the crew busy. The few yards they managed to gain in no way altered their predicament. Now and then, the ice tantalized them: a lead would suddenly develop. But then, almost at once, it closed back up. The pack played cat and mouse with the ship that it would never again release.

Time was running out for Shackleton. He had wanted to go ashore for a long time; now, in February, he had to admit that winter was just around the corner, something that ruled out the question of leaving the ship. They had drifted 60 nautical miles along the coast, but it never entered Shackleton's mind to leave ship and men alone in this situation. While depots were feverishly being set up for the Pole group on McMurdo Sound on the other side of Antarctica, the overall project had failed before it had properly begun. More tragic still was the fact that the AURORA group, who had to wait over two years for their return, faring little better than the crew of the ENDURANCE, lost three people. The story of AURORA runs a close second to that of ENDURANCE for excitement and drama.

But the focal point for the public has always been Shackleton and ENDURANCE, so the sufferings of the AURORA party are largely unknown. The Antarctic claimed its victims.

The icebound ship and men drifted in a northwesterly direction into the center of the maelstrom. On board EN-DURANCE preparations were being made for staying over the winter. Seals and penguins were hunted; even the dogs were trained on the ice. Shackleton did his level best to keep the men busy and weld them together as a group. Despite the wretched situation, morale was surprisingly high. It was clear that the expedition had gone awry but Shackleton was now in his element.

Everyone aboard, Shackelton most of all, sensed that this was only the start of their travails. Accordingly, he used all his skill to keep the men in good spirits and in good health; he endeavored to get them out of their predicament and bring them home safely.

That winter and in the following spring, heavy pressure set in, throwing the ENDURANCE back and forth like a cork. Only thanks to her incredibly stout construction was she spared from destruction.

There is something terribly dramatic and eerie about pressure ice. I have experienced this a number of times aboard my boat, DAGMAR AAEN. a North Sea cutter. Once, I even came very close to losing her that way. The pressure exerted by the ice becomes so enormous that a vessel's only hope lies in escaping upwards, by having a hull that gives the ice nothing to grab onto. We got off cheaply—just one splintered plank, the rudder assembly destroyed, and a terrific fright. But none of us will ever forget the elemental power of the ice.

The pressure conditions in the Weddell Sea must have been unparalleled in magnitude. Reading Shackleton's account, we find that the deck beams and planking bowed and buckled upwards; the forces exerted must have been incredible, considering the strength of ENDURANCE's hull. Perhaps the FRAM, designed for drifting in ice, might have withstood the pressure. ENDURANCE, because of the large deadrise angle of her hull, was stuck and never managed to escape the danger zone. She resisted with all her might but, on October 24, crushing forces developed that Shackleton described as "the beginning of the end."

The death of ENDURANCE was slow and agonizing. She did not just disappear. On October 27, the exhausted men were ordered to rig pumps in the bilges to stem the inrush of sea water. ENDURANCE was now a listing wreck. Though she might stay afloat for some time, it was no longer safe for the men to stay aboard. Their hopes for reaching open water and getting home seemed lost with the ship. Shackleton's men were in one of the most inaccessible and inhospitable regions of the earth. The prospects for rescue were virtually non-existent.

3

A Grave Decision

Some say that it was fortunate for Shackleton and his men that they could not set out on their planned crossing of the Antarctic Continent. Their chances of coming through would have been exceedingly slim, despite the fact that he was using the only viable strategy—one that included food and fuel depots set up from the other side of the continent.

The same tactic was employed successfully by Vivian Fuchs, an Englishman, during his 1957/58 expedition. With eight tracked vehicles, sleds and two dogsleds he left from Shackleton Base—the very place Sir Ernest had picked for a starting point. At the same time, another party under the command of Sir Edmund Hillary, the first man to conquer Mount Everest, started from the Ross Sea; this party was to set a trail with tracked vehicles for Vivian Fuchs's group. Hillary would be the first person to reach the South Pole since Scott. Of course, Hillary had massive technical support and a huge pool of vehicles. The plan worked, if only because of all the technical and logistical backup (which included airplanes).

It was not until 1989/90 that Reinhold Messner and I crossed the continent—Shackleton-style. We had a single depot set up for us in the area of the Thiel Mountains, halfway to the South Pole, and a second one at the Pole itself. We were able to cross Antarctica then and conduct other expeditions since, largely thanks to modern, ultra-lightweight materials as well as carefully tailored nutritional plans. None of this was available in Shackleton's day. Sleds then were made of heavy wood and not "baked" of laminated Kevlar and carbon fiber. The scourge of scurvy has been eradicated since the advent of multi-vitamin pills.

Carbohydrates, minerals, egg whites and fat were available to us at all times in well-balanced proportions and adequate quantities. At the end of our trek we were both a few pounds lighter and, from a nutritional standpoint, we were healthier and had a better diet than at home. With all due respect for Shackleton's ability, I doubt that a crossing in his time would have succeeded, given the materials available. In my opinion, the concerns of some critics of the Imperial Trans-Antarctic Expedition cannot be dismissed. Instead of the hoped-for triumph, it could well have become another national disaster like Scott's. At any rate, around this time there were very different concerns: World War I had begun.

But the castaways knew nothing about the war.

As they left the smashed ENDURANCE and set up the first camp on the ice, Shackleton called on his men to discard all non-essentials. To make his point, he pulled from his pockets several gold coins along with his gold cigarette case and tossed them into the snow. Then he produced the Bible which Queen Alexandra had presented to him when they sailed from England. She had made the following inscription.

"For the crew of the ENDURANCE from Alexandra, May 31, 1914.

"May the Lord help you to do your duty and guide you through all dangers by land and sea. May you see all the works of the Lord and all his wonders in the deep."

Shackleton tore out a page from the Book of Job and laid the Bible next to the other things on the snow. Later, one of the men recovered the Bible and kept it with him throughout the journey.

Shackleton knew that weight would be a serious factor when they eventually took to the lifeboats, his only hope of getting the men to Paulet Island 346 miles away. There was a house there, as well as a food depot from a previous expedition led by Otto Nordenskjöld who, a few years before, had also lost his ship, the ANTARCTIC, and had been forced to spend the winter on the island. Another party belonging to the same expedition had erected a hut at Hope Bay—today, the Argentinian Esperanza Station.

Paulet Island was nearer, and it had food. Shackleton saw right away the one snag in the plan. The island could be reached only by sea—not over the ice. If they did manage to reach Paulet and meant to go for help from there, it would require the lifeboats. Since the boats had been taken off the ENDURANCE just in time, the only question was how they would be transported. Shackleton put up to fifteen men in harness in front of a sled on which one lifeboat had been loaded. After about half a mile, he stopped them and sent them back for the second boat. Then the third. All three of the wooden lifeboats being of heavy construction, the men were soon at the end of their strength.

Ahead of them lay a jumble of shattered ice with huge up-ended floes standing fifteen feet high. By the evening of their second day camped on an ice floe, Shackleton recognized the futility of their efforts. They had gained barely two miles since leaving the ship, and the remains of the wreck were still clearly in sight. The strategy had to be changed. From now on, they would wait. Since their gigantic, level ice floe offered them safety from the ice jam, they would use it to let their camp drift as far north as possible—until the lifeboats could be launched. Making themselves as comfortable as possible, they called this place "Ocean Camp."

From then on, their days were marked by routine and idleness. They cooked, they repaired equipment; they hunted seals and penguins. At this time, McNeish, the ship's carpenter, began to strengthen the lifeboats. Pouring his energy into this work, he raised their freeboard, decked them over bow and stern, then reinforced their stems to withstand collisions with ice.

McNeish, a dour, rather taciturn individual, was a master at his craft. It was only much later that it was realized just how vital his boatbuilding efforts at Ocean Camp had been, at a time when lumber and materials from the wreck were still available. Actually, McNeish's energy and skill were at least as crucial in the subsequent rescue as Shackleton's own courage. So it becomes hard to fathom why, after their return to England, Shackleton would withhold the Polar Medal from— among others—the ship's carpenter. Shackleton held a grudge against McNeish, one he could not rid himself of even in the hour of triumph. Be this as it may, one thing remains certain: Without McNeish's boatbuilding work, the two smaller lifeboats STANCOMB WILLS and DUDLEY DOCKER would never have survived the journey to Elephant Island.

Life on the ice floe grew more and more monotonous. Some men's morale sank even lower—including Shackleton's, who suffered from sciatica and, at times, was confined to his tent. Now there were open discussions about whether the Boss's decisions had been right. When, on December 23, he gave the order to strike camp and move everything farther onto the ice, some people argued against it openly and vehemently. Shackleton won out but since they had only progressed eight miles after a week of backbreaking exertions, he again broke off the march. He had them establish a second camp that would bear the name of "Patience Camp." And patience was really what the crew needed.

Again and again, McNeish—or, in sailor's parlance "Chippy"—set about repairing the planking of the lifeboats damaged on the march. For want of oakum or tar, he used lampwick and penguin blood to caulk the seams of their hulls.

Since leaving the ENDURANCE, the food supplies were dwindling. Under these drastically straitened circumstances, three puppies had to be shot. McNeish was told to shoot his cat, Mrs. Chippy, something for which he never forgave Shackleton.

February heralded the end of the Antarctic summer. The weather grew worse and worse; the temperature fell sharply. The men's clothing and the sleeping bags were scarcely warm enough to protect them from the deteriorating weather. At the beginning of March, the temperature dropped so far beneath the freezing point that the sleeping bags became as stiff as boards. Sleep was now impossible.

On March 7 they noticed a peculiar movement to the ice. The floe on which they were camped began a rocking motion, an unmistakable sign of ground swell. Because ice floes have a pronounced cushioning effect, the ground swell cannot travel very far in the ice. The men knew this and it became apparent that their period adrift on the ice was nearing an end. Their floe held up until, on April 9, the ice cracked so wide open that they had to launch the lifeboats.

In the swells of the open sea the three-foot-thick floes rose and fell, crashing into one another like freight cars in a marshalling yard; they split in half, forming ever newer floes. Any boat caught between two of them would have been smashed like an empty matchbox. It was here—not on Elephant Island—that the boat journey of Shackleton and his men began.

Days earlier they had sighted land in the west—apparently, large Joinville Island that lies next to Paulet Island. But the drift had already carried them so far north that they would pass the islands before reaching open water. They had overshot their goal and were now being driven by the current into the open sea.

They had already been wandering on the ice for well over a year. But the dangers and hardships to come, in the lifeboats among ice floes, would far eclipse what they had endured thus far. The cold, the wet, and the constant fear of being crushed by the swaying, omnipresent floes would bring them to the brink of physical and mental exhaustion. At night they bivouacked on the floes, drifting fearfully close to gigantic icebergs which, like icebreakers, plowed through the fields of pack ice.

Rain and snow reduced the visibility. In addition, the ocean currents dealt them a low blow: Although they had been trying for the South Shetland Islands, the current was carrying them off course. Now they were further south than when they had first taken to the boats. The whalers had warned them about the currents.

When the wind finally swung around to the southeast,

they were so tired that Shackleton feared some of them might not survive. Only Elephant or Clarence Islands lay within their reach. No one knew if a safe landing could be made on either island. The storm-tossed sea swamped the lifeboats continuously, so that the men had to bail for their lives. Some became delirious, unable to speak a word. If they did not reach land very soon, a number of them—like young Black-borow whose feet were badly frostbitten—would not live another day. The journey became a race with death.

Squalls alternated with heavy fog as they approached Elephant Island. Only when the scarves of fog lifted were they able to determine that they were right off Cape Valentine, cold, forbidding and barren-looking. The JAMES CAIRD and the STANCOMB WILLS were linked by a towline; the DUDLEY DOCKER, on its own, sometimes dropped out of sight. A landing on this steep coast would be an act of total desperation. But any patch of dry land, anything was better than their wretched existence in the open boats.

All three lifeboats made it through the surf to a narrow strip of gravel beach. Before the heavy JAMES CAIRD could be dragged ashore, the exhausted men had to unload her in the breakers. Some of them stumbled around as if drunk. Exhaustion, cold, hunger and thirst had driven them nearly mad. The crew of the little STANCOMB WILLS had suffered worst of all. Some were totally unresponsive; others filled their pockets with pebbles as if with gold. Still another grabbed an axe and began slaughtering the seals lying on the beach. For a week they had huddled in the open boats on the ocean. For the first time since leaving South Georgia 497 days before, there was solid ground under their feet. They had lost their ship, drifted in pack ice for months, and survived a harrowing ocean journey. Now they stood on a strip of gravel beach a few yards wide. In bad weather, it would be submerged right up to the base of the granite walls behind them. The cliffs themselves were steep and craggy; rock slides started in places. Sooner or later, the men would either be engulfed by the angry sea or crushed by falling rock. Even in their state, they realized they could not stay there.

The very next morning, Shackleton sent out the DUDLEY DOCKER under Frank Wild's command to search for a better campsite. The party did not return until after nightfall. Wild had found a place seven miles down the coast that promised more protection than Cape Valentine. The following day, the entire party set out in the boats to occupy the new campsite. But the weather turned vicious. Before they reached the landing place, katabatic winds overtook them, nearly capsizing the DUDLEY DOCKER. Sailing the open boats this short distance—and under the lee of the land—had been a struggle for survival. As the three boats were pulled ashore, Shackleton glanced around and remarked that the spit of land was "by no means an ideal camping ground." But it was better than Cape Valentine and, he thought, the best they would find on that coast.

This in no way meant the end of their sufferings, however. Winter was approaching once more. They could not expect any whaling ship to stray into this part of the ocean. All those vessels were long gone, they would not return to the region until the following summer. The marooned men would never be able to hold out that long. Even if they did, there was absolutely no guarantee of being sighted on Elephant Island.

The castaways had to take their fate in their own hands. Shackleton was preparing a plan to do just that.

4

Island in the Storm

It is foggy and drizzling as the Hapag Lloyd cruise ship HANSEATIC slowly approaches the bleak backdrop of Elephant Island in the early morning hours of January 11, 2000.

As I stand on the bridge, it all seems like a movie. Protected from the wind and the cold by the bridge windows, I study the glacial moraines, the snow cornices and the ice flowers formed on the peaks by gale-force winds. Dark, sinister-looking cliffs rise starkly from the foamy surf, as if this Antarctic island wanted to resist any landing attempts—and it does resist them. But for the long ground swell, which manages to make itself felt on a stabilizer-equipped liner as big as the HANSEATIC, I might be sitting in the movies staring at a panoramic screen. It is quiet on the bridge. Besides Captain Thilo Natke and First Officer Sven Gärtner, there is a Filipino helmsman as well as a few early risers from among the passengers. The radar screen clearly shows the contours of Point Wild and its bay. This is the moment I have been waiting for.

As we boarded the HANSEATIC in the Argentinian port of Ushuaia, the long preliminary and planning phase came to a close. About a year before, I had contacted Bärbel Krämer of Hapag Lloyd about the expedition I was planning.

"You want to re-enact Shackleton's journey?" Her question was more of a statement. She sounded incredulous.

"Yes, I mean to do it using a perfect replica of the JAMES CAIRD. I had the boat built at Christian Jonsson's boatyard in Denmark. In terms of logistics, our biggest problem is shipping the JAMES CAIRD II to the Antarctic. Would it be possible for the HANSEATIC to take boat and crew to the starting point and drop us there?"

There was a silence and then she replied: "Why not?"

A great weight fell from my shoulders. Naturally, Hapag Lloyd would have to discuss the project internally but, shortly after the phone conversation, I got the green light from the Hamburg office. One less headache.

While the HANSEATIC was undergoing a routine check at a Bremerhaven shipyard a few weeks later, I had the opportunity to get to know ship and crew. At first I wasn't sure how the ship's officers were going to take this kind of venture— with their knowledge of the prevailing conditions in Antarctica they might consider the whole project totally absurd. I was therefore extremely pleased that Captain Natke and First Officer Gärtner received the idea enthusiastically. They immediately assigned a spot for stowing the boat. With sketch pads, the blueprints of the JAMES CAIRD II, and tape measures, we studied how the boat could be hoisted into place— and, all at once, we were down to the nitty-gritty in the planning.

Leaving the shipyard, I was overjoyed. I had not only

found a solution to the problem of getting the boat to Antarctica, but had also met the ship's incredibly friendly officers who were willing to cooperate as much as possible.

Since first stumbling across the JAMES CAIRD at the exhibit in Bonn, I had known she was real. But blueprints for her no longer existed. So one of us flew straight to New York where the boat was at another exhibit and, with the consent of the owners—Dulwich College—took her measurements and lines. Next on the agenda: Helmut Radebold, engineer at the Hamburg firm of naval architects Schiffko, fed the data into the computer and a new JAMES CAIRD was reconstructed.

Helmut is a perfectionist. He set to work with the same accuracy, the same painstaking care he would use in building an 800-foot containership.

As I looked over his shoulder in amazement, her lines appeared on the computer screen. I watched as endless columns of figures—incomprehensible for me—tallied with each other. Even before the boat's keel was laid, Helmut could tell how she would sail and what her sea-going qualities were like. I even had the feeling that he no longer needed to see the original boat. He'd memorized it all after seeing the results of the first tests.

But that wasn't all. To expedite the work, he plotted the lines at a scale of 1:1—an incredible economy of labor for the boatbuilder. Armed with this, we were off to Christian Jonsson's yard, in the town of Egernsund, Denmark. In my mind, there had been no question of having the replica of the JAMES CAIRD executed by anyone but Christian and his men. When a project like this is at stake, boatbuilding becomes a matter of trust. For twelve years I had been bringing my North Sea cutter DAGMAR AAEN to Christian and, if she had withstood pressure ice and gales, it was largely due to the painstaking, rock-solid workmanship at his yard. With this project, too, I sensed his earnestness and conscientiousness right from Day One.

During the building phase I didn't have the time to constantly monitor work on the boat. I just put myself entirely in Christian's hands and the job went better than if I had kept talking to him non-stop. I do the sailing—not the boatbuilding. Accurate self-appraisal is the first step to success. I restrained myself and left the field to Christian and Helmut. That way, a new JAMES CAIRD was ready in the summer of 1999. Working under Christian, Carl Jörgensen played a pivotal role in the building of the boat.

At about this time, Professor Günter Grabe, dean of Kiel Technical College, who, for years, had been researching the design of the rig, came up with the layout for the masts and sails, as well as the standing and running rigging. Painstakingly, he studied all written material pertaining to the rigging of the original JAMES CAIRD. As far as we know, he kept to the original dimensions and, where no information could be had, he bridged the gaps using the principle of the greatest probability.

Although our timetable was extremely tight, we celebrated the launching on October 2. In a festive ceremony, the tops of her masts dressed with signal flags, her gunwales festooned with garlands of flowers, the JAMES CAIRD II—as she would henceforth be known—slid down the ways to the applause of many guests as well as Christian's yard crew. Moments earlier, Brigitte, my sweetheart, had cracked the traditional bottle of champagne over the bow. The pretty double-ended replica was afloat. Even before we had her properly made fast to the pier, Carl sprang aboard to see if she was really tight. Barely discernible, a couple of drops of water trickled in at one spot. It was really nothing, but Carl was beside himself. The next day, he had the boat hauled out again and got that seam re-caulked. There was simply no arguing with him.

Directly astern of JAMES CAIRD II bobbed DAGMAR AAEN, at the yard for a general overhaul. The decision had been made meanwhile to have IFAGE, a television production company, shoot several documentary films in the course of the expedition. Unlike the tiny JAMES CAIRD II, the DAGMAR AAEN would be making the passage to the Antarctic on her own. For this, not only did she need to be fitted out and overhauled, but she also had to be on her way very soon. Martin Friederichs, a recent graduate in geography and a longtime companion on different expeditions, would be skippering the old girl. But he was also earmarked for a berth on the JAMES CAIRD II. After we found a replacement for him in Ushuaia, Argentina, he would transfer over to the JAMES CAIRD II.

So that everything would go according to plan, we had to keep to our schedule. In the days that followed, we worked like madmen to get the DAGMAR AAEN ready. On October 14, we transited the Kiel Canal and, that same evening, I went ashore in the port of Brunsbüttel after turning the cutter over to Martin. What a strange feeling! Not because of Martin—he had already skippered my 50-foot yacht a number of times and a better seaman would be hard to find. No, it was the first time that the DAGMAR AAEN had ever set out on a voyage from our homeport—without me aboard. I was in a strange mood and, on leaving them, I never once turned to look back. She sailed the next day while I gave a press conference in Hamburg aimed at bringing the new expedition to the attention of the general public. No going back now—the starting flag was down. By this time, the DAGMAR AAEN was already somewhere in the North Sea. Facing her was a voyage of roughly 24,000 nautical miles roundtrip, a voyage that would take up to eleven months.

Between lectures, press deadlines, and the stowing of various gear, we put the JAMES CAIRD II through her shakedown. The whole crew had been assembled for the first time at the launching to get our replica of Shackleton's boat ready and, most of all, to sail her. One crewmember would be Sigga (her full name is Sigridur Ragna Sverrisdottir) from Iceland, with us on a regular basis since 1995. Among other things, she had taken charge of the DAGMAR AAEN staying over the winter in Scoresby Sound, East Greenland. Nothing in the world could have kept her away from this new expedition. At first, I had tried to keep Sigga from going but soon gave in. Not that I lacked confidence in her for the trip, on the contrary. I knew this was to be a very dangerous voyage, we would be living in extremely cramped quarters—and we would have no toilet facilities. She swept all my objections aside with a torrent of words and she was on the team.

Along with Martin, Sigga and myself, Henryk Wolski joined us as the fourth member of the team. Henryk is a Pole who has lived in Germany for about twenty years and, since 1992, has been sailing on the DAGMAR AAEN a good deal of the time. Among other trips, he was with us in Russia during the ICESAIL Expedition and helped sail the DAGMAR AAEN through the Northwest Passage. He owns a replica of a Viking ship in which he has made some long trips. In addition, he works as a sailing instructor and heads up the firm Sachen Segeln.

There were going to be the four of us—two fewer than in the original boat. Later on, we often tried to figure out how Shackleton had managed to cram six men into a boat that size. Even with just us four, plus gear, the boat seemed filled to capacity.

On November 8 the boat was delivered on a trailer to Hamburg. Pro Freight, the company that has always met our hauling needs in the most godforsaken corners of the globe, came through for us once again. And this time Boje Paulsen, the company's owner, insisted on supervising the loading himself. Fully equipped, JAMES CAIRD II, carefully supported by lots of wooden pallets, was traveling in a 40-foot cargo container. Various lashings held the boat in position. Boje made one last inspection, and then the doors swung shut. Two days later, the container was offloaded and, via Buenos Aires, would reach Ushuaia shortly before Christmas.

On December 29, Sigga, Henryk and Brigitte flew to South America. Torsten Heller and I followed. Brigitte and Torsten were both working as photographers and would make the trip down there on the HANSEATIC. When Torsten later transferred to the DAGMAR AAEN, Brigitte would bring back to Germany all the film thus far exposed.

We celebrated the Millennium and New Year's Eve in Ushuaia. At the peak of its summer season, the town served up a huge fireworks display. On January 2, the DAGMAR AAEN arrived in port. A hurricane in Le Maire Strait had hit them so hard they'd been forced to turn and run from it. Martin could not remember having ever seen seas that high and this—coming from a man generally given to understatement—meant something. Cape Horn was sending its first stormy greetings and giving them a foretaste of the Antarctic journey that lay in store. In addition, damage to the propeller shaft made it necessary for us to haul the cutter out. The only drydock in Ushuaia belonged to the Argentinian Navy and they immediately offered to help. Our machinist, Egon Fogtmann, a Dane, set to work with the necessary spare parts that arrived on the first plane. Wearing coveralls, he was soon busy at the drydock, removing the DAGMAR AAEN's prop and replacing the shaft. He and the crew worked in a torrential downpour while, a stone's-throw away, on the other side of the pier, the cargo container holding the JAMES CAIRD II was being swung off the HANSEATIC.

I watched with bated breath as the doors of the container were opened. When I saw the boat standing there exactly as she had looked in Hamburg, I resumed breathing normally again. The rest all seemed to go terribly fast. A crane set the boat down into the harbor basin, a Zodiac from the HANSEATIC towed her alongside the cruise ship, and Sven Gärtner with his people took care of the rest. A few minutes later, the CAIRD II again sat high and dry in the between-decks of the luxury liner below the lifeboats, lashed down to stand any weather. There was hardly time left to say goodbye to the crew of the DAGMAR AAEN who, covered with tar and grease, were still hard at work in the drydock.

We were the last passengers to board the HANSEATIC. Soaked to the skin and still wearing coveralls, we fled to our cabins to begin trying to adapt to reality on board. Since we were now passengers aboard a floating five-star hotel, we would have to conform. The last few days had been so turbulent that we still couldn't grasp the fact that everything had actually gone off on schedule. Even as I sat blissfully in the bathtub scrubbing the dirt off my hands and arms, the

HANSEATIC was heading for the Falkland Islands. From there the cruise ship went in the direction of Elephant Island—which is looming up full size ahead of us right now.

In the five days since leaving Ushuaia, we have developed a warm friendship with Thilo and Sven, as well as with Bettina Schlennstedt, who looks after the passengers. Thilo and Sven want to help me get at least a look at Point Wild. Weather permitting, we will even attempt a landing there.

A few hours later, Sven and I are seated in the big Zodiac racing toward the coast. The island's gloom and desolation are heightened by incessant rain and wind. Thundering surf crashes against the endless cliffs and, from the rocky beach, the wind carries the stench of the penguin rookery. We are lying directly off the breakers at the spit of land called Point Wild. There, Shackleton and his men established their camp. Sven wants to get us in there, but sees that a landing today is really out of the question. Sven has already been there several times. "It's very seldom possible to land here," he tells me. Somehow it all seems unreal: jumping from the warmth and security of the HANSEATIC into a Zodiac with its big outboard motor to study these perpendicular granite walls up close. Mentally, this is a real quantum leap. But I get a good overview of the terrain, something that will help us later on when we are shooting for our landfall in the JAMES CAIRD II.

At Cape Valentine, Sven and I repeat the exercise. The weather becomes so bad that the inflatable leaps—rather than slides—over the crests of waves. Now, after going only a few yards, we can no longer make out the HANSEATIC, as fog, snow and hail reduce visibility. Cape Valentine offers the same picture as Point Wild: thundering surf and a strip of beach so narrow that I wonder how Shackleton and his men managed to get ashore dry-shod—I seriously doubt that they could. Behind the beach rise vertical granite cliffs from which rocks the size of a man's fist pelt down continuously. Once more, we cannot land. The place looks even more bleak and desolate than Point Wild. No wonder Shackleton cleared out of this spot as soon as possible. But if we remember that the castaways had been overjoyed to reach land, we can guess how just terrible their journey must have been.

Sven steers the inflatable around a rock, coming so close I could almost jump ashore. I decide to give it a miss and a while later am really glad to see the HANSEATIC heave into view. She welcomes us back with all her comfort and security. As soon as we are aboard, the ship resumes her cruise. The objective now is Cape Lookout, a somewhat sheltered spot lying about 19 miles from Cape Valentine. Despite the fact that the weather is still rather bad, the ship's crew manages to ferry all the passengers ashore making sure that none of them gets too close to where seals lie or penguins brood. Why, I kept wondering on my brief stay ashore, hadn't Shackleton landed *here*? This bay is considerably more sheltered than Point Wild. Wouldn't it have made more sense to reconnoiter the island first and, possibly, look for alternatives before making themselves at home? In fact, was the voyage to South Georgia—that game of Russian roulette—actually necessary? For a long time I had regarded Shackleton's course of action as the only possibility. Now, suddenly, I began to ponder the question. Could there have been alternatives?

5

Esperanza – Hope Bay

On the morning of January 12, the HANSEATIC reaches Paulet Island. Her engines stopped, the ship lies among fields of pack ice while Zodiacs, like busy ants, ply between the land and the luxury liner, ferrying passengers ashore. On a small hill, amid thousands of penguins, lay the ruins of a hut that Shackleton had originally meant to reach. It was first built by the castaways of the ANTARCTIC and, in Shackleton's time, the building must have still represented an imposing structure. In those days, a supply of food was stored there; in addition, the waters were simply teeming with seals and penguins. Clearly, had the men of the ENDURANCE managed to get here, they would have had a far better jumping-off point than the one they found on Elephant Island. They might have stayed on—and, if necessary, survived the winter there. Then, with favorable winds, they could have easily made the Antarctic Peninsula. The chances of encountering a ship in this region were far greater than at Elephant Island. Yet the weather and the ice drift had decreed another fate for the castaways.

The visit to Elephant Island, even in an inflatable, made me more curious than ever. This has nothing to do with shattering myths. In all the literature on the ENDURANCE expedition apparently no one having the necessary expertise went to the trouble of critically examining the sequence of events and the decisions taken. At least, I know of no such approach. For some people, criticizing Shackleton is sacrilege. In my opinion, understanding his decision-making processes makes for a more interesting study than merely rehashing the same old story ad infinitum. That was the thought behind our expedition. A fair and meaningful assessment of the Shackleton expedition can only be made by approximating the conditions he faced as closely as possible. It may be convenient to make judgments from the safety of a heated office, but safety is one thing and fairness another. By eliminating distance and gaining the clearest possible insight into the decision-making process, we might be able to unearth new facts.

For us, today means saying goodbye to the HANSEATIC, to comfort, to security, to everything people consider indispensable on a visit to the polar regions. We will voluntarily put ourselves in the position of castaways. Granted, however, without having to share their desperation. We too will experience desperate moments and get a taste of being terribly wet and cold. But we won't know the fear Shackleton's men had—the fear of never being found, of never being rescued. Lots of people know where we are; they know our plans. By contrast, the men of the ENDURANCE were presumed lost and only a few in far-off England were still hoping for rescue. At any rate, help from the outside was out of the question.

Is it cynical to place yourself voluntarily in the position of desperate men whose only thought was of reaching home safely? Is this the kick adventurers fleeing civilization need, the way a junkie needs his shot? I have often wondered: "How far should I go, how much should I expose myself and my companions to danger?" From a moral standpoint this trip is also a balancing act. I go on expeditions because they give me something positive, not because I have a masochistic streak. This entails a tolerance for hardship and a fatalistic component—not as an end in itself but, rather, the means to an end. In addition, I believe that my companions and I are capable of making this journey.

I am quite used to the polar landscape. I, too, have spent weeks drifting on an ice floe, without the possibility of reaching land. I understand snow, ice and the cold, know the danger of icebergs and, without wishing to be presumptuous, have in the past twenty years logged as much time in polar ice as Shackleton. Much that seems terribly dangerous to an outsider is quite routine for my companions and me. Thanks to this collective know-how and myriad built-in safety systems the journey seemed defensible—albeit, for me, the trip was at the upper limits of justifiable risk. Henryk, Sigga and Martin see things the same way and did not make their decision lightly. We thoroughly discussed the possible dangers before jointly reaching the same conclusion: it had to be done with this team. Should we succeed in making this journey, we would have a different story to tell than the historians who rely on yellowing journals and records for their sources.

In the clear, crisp air, the distances shrink. Islands far away stand out clearly in the gloriously blue sky. They seem to be within reach. It is a flat calm—no comparison with the dreadful weather we had just yesterday. That is also typical for Antarctica—the weather changes quickly and, often, quite unpredictably. Today the landscape seems peaceful and picturesque. There are ice floes on which seals wallow sluggishly in the sun. Droves of penguins waddle back and forth, as if terribly busy.

North of tiny Paulet Island lie the larger Dundee and Joinville Islands whose ice caps seem sugar frosted, glistening in the sunlight. On the trip into Hope Bay, the HANSEATIC, with her reinforced bow, must batter a path through the ice fields several times. Whenever her stem splits an ice floe several feet thick, vibrations run through the vessel. The Antarctic Sound, through which we are traveling, is full of icebergs and pack-ice fields.

We complete the final preparations. At 2 p.m. the HANSEATIC enters Esperanza Bay and soon we make out the red houses of the Argentinian research station. The wind rises—abruptly, as is typical for Antarctica. We work feverishly with the Filipino deckhands and Sven Gärtner to lower the JAMES CAIRD II into the water. Passengers, watching us descend from deck to deck, wish us well, their cameras and Camcorders clicking and whirring. Captain Thilo Natke, who has been briefed about our projected scheduling and route—as well as our contingency plans—does not join us on the deck of the pitching double-ender. Everything must go quickly now. The wind has freshened and the JAMES CAIRD II, like a high-strung prima ballerina, dances and gyrates at the base of HANSEATIC's motionless bulk. If the replica is this tender now, how is she going to behave in our first real storm? Coming over, even the huge HANSEATIC pitched and rolled in the open ocean. How will our tiny craft stand up out there?

Sigga and Henryk fill the water tanks and now we sense that our motion has slowed down a tad. The tanks serve not only as our supply of drinking water but also as ballast, being located at the lowest point of the boat. Martin, Sven and I step both masts and stay them temporarily. From his Zodiac, Sven also gets a towline aboard us.

Finally we are ready. A last handshake, then I stand on the forward deck hanging onto the mainmast while Sigga takes the helm, and Sven starts towing us slowly. Wearing my light fleece jacket, I am soaked to the skin in less than two minutes. The wind sends the spray flying high and I haven't found yet my sea-legs for this kind of a journey—besides wearing the wrong gear. Behind me is the white mass of the HANSEATIC. A starker contrast between two vessels is inconceivable. Over there are the comfort and warmth of a floating luxury hotel; here, the maritime stone age.

I never had a chance to say goodbye to Brigitte; somehow everything went too fast. In her yellow oilies, she waves to me from a Zodiac that is making a bee-line for the HANSEATIC. How I wish I were holding her in my arms! Instead, I'm hugging the stupid mast and suddenly feeling terribly alone. Then she's gone. She will make the trip back in the HANSEATIC and, from Ushuaia, she will fly home with the film and photo equipment. Brigitte is an accomplished sailor herself and has a number of expeditions to her credit. She also knows her own limits. The journey in the JAMES CAIRD II is not for her. Had it been the DAGMAR AAEN, Brigitte would have sailed with us in a minute. Even our planned crossing of South Georgia fascinated her. But in this instance there is a time constraint—some other day we'll return and explore these places together.

At the research station there is only a small dilapidated pier. By radio, Thilo asks Sven to come back aboard right away, as the cruise ship must keep to her schedule. I'm still standing on deck, dazed and soaking wet. A final "Good luck and good sailing!" from Sven and then we are alone.

At once, the JAMES CAIRD II monopolizes our attention. Her stem is being pounded badly against a submerged rock. In a flash, Henryk, Sigga and Torsten are ashore with a line out forward. If I can manage to find the end of my fouled line in the cockpit, I may be able to get an anchor over the stern. Somehow this is starting all wrong. We've got to do better than this. When the boat is finally secure and I get ashore, we all begin breathing normally. The Argentinians have assigned us a vacant hut right at the foot of the pier where we can pitch camp for the next few days. By now, the DAGMAR AAEN must be somewhere in the stormy Drake Passage, so it will be several days before she puts in here. At any rate, we still have plenty to do.

While we busy ourselves with the boat in the days that follow, we keep receiving visits from curious Adelie penguins. Right next-door to the station is a huge rookery full of white shirt-fronts. Humans and penguins apparently live here together in harmony. Anyway, we bump into these little fellows all over the place. Our arrival seems to have a certain entertainment value for them. Alone, in pairs, or in whole groups, they come pitter-pattering onto the dock to watch us at work, craning their necks upwards with interest, whispering and talking to one another—who knows what about.

The Argentinians make no attempt to conceal the fact that they consider us lunatics, but do their utmost to make our "last days" as pleasant as possible. They allow us to use their showers and keep inviting us over for meals. They look very distressed when we assure them that we have everything we need and that we must gratefully decline their offer of extra food for the journey.

Near our base camp stand the crudely built walls of an old hut. Its roof has collapsed but, apart from that, it looks fairly good. This hut was erected by the same ill-fated expedition that built the house on Paulet Island. Another group of the ANTARCTIC expedition stayed over the winter before finally being rescued by an Argentinian search party.

Shackleton knew about the hut on Esperanza Bay. Even if it was too small for 28 men, there was enough building material there and, most importantly, food in the form of seals and penguins. In addition, a search party would almost certainly call at such a place to see if anyone from the missing expedition were there. The Antarctic is incredibly vast. There is only a remote possibility of being found by mere chance somewhere in these waters. Men who are lost must either head for a known point where search parties would look or take destiny in their own hands—Shackleton decided on the latter course.

While Torsten drags camera and video equipment around to record our every move, Sigga, Henryk and I get the JAMES CAIRD II ready. To accustom ourselves to the boat's cramped quarters and motion, we move out of the hut and start sleeping on board. That way, every handhold will be learned, all our movements coordinated. With the replica fully loaded with food and equipment, there is little room to spare. How the devil did our predecessors cram six in here? There are still only the three of us and we wonder how we will squeeze in Martin, the fourth member of the crew.

Somehow everything falls into place. On the evening of January 16 I spot the gaff-rigged DAGMAR AAEN in the distance, just entering Esperanza Bay. The cutter moves purposefully our way, and it all seems the most natural thing in the world. It is in fact anything but. She's had to weather another gale in the Drake Passage, not to mention that she's almost on schedule at the other end of the earth after a 8,895-mile voyage. Now the IFAGE camera crew is also on board the DAGMAR AAEN in order to film the expedition for German television. Georg Graffe and Ralf Gemmecke are old friends of mine. We know each other from an earlier expedition to Spitsbergen where we lived and worked together.

The third and newest member of the team is Tim Schneider, the camera assistant. Aside from the comparatively calm and sheltered waters at Spitsbergen and a summer tour on the Adriatic, none of the three has any real sailing experience. Tim's experience is limited to exactly one ferry ride to Helgoland, the North Sea resort. I can only marvel at the courage and determination of these three tyros braving Drake Passage their first time out—and that's merely the beginning. In addition to their film assignments, they stand watch, cook and pull their weight like the rest. Sailing is not their passion, something that makes their work on board even more commendable. After this trip is over, they won't have anything much to learn about ocean voyages, about gales, about being wet and cold. Two months aboard a 50-foot cutter in the Southern Ocean—that's about the ultimate sailing adventure.

In Ushuaia, Martin turned over command to Karsten Steinbach, who will skipper the DAGMAR AAEN until the end of the expedition. In everyday life, Karsten is a flight captain with Condor and Lufthansa Airlines. He has been sailing since early childhood. There are only two people to whom I would entrust the DAGMAR AAEN—particularly, in this part of the ocean. Martin is one, Karsten the other. Karsten contributes tremendous professionalism and vision in all respects. He, like Martin, is a dyed-in-the-wool sailor. They know each other from the Kiel University Sailing Association where they act as skippers for the PETER VON DANZIG.

Today must be something really special for Martin. He is the only one of us four to have sailed all the way down here from Germany, to participate in the journey of the JAMES CAIRD II. And he will be the only one of us to sail back home. To do that means being at sea continuously for up to eleven months. But that doesn't bother him. Far from it. With his calm, pragmatic turn of mind, and his irrepressible humor, he soon manages to cope with the CAIRD's cramped quarters.

For the first time in a long, long while, we are sitting together quietly. On January 18 the JAMES CAIRD II is ready for sea. The following day, we will set out—almost 84 years after Shackleton.

6

The Gamble

We feel apprehension as our hazardous undertaking draws near. I have seldom been so worried or slept so badly on the eve of any other voyage. I am just plain scared. Not enough to make me abandon the project but sufficiently to give me some sleepless nights. Even during the daytime, somewhere in the back of my mind are thoughts about the journey and its possible dangers. It's been like this for weeks, months. Martin, Henryk and Sigga feel the same way. We often discuss the fear and try to channel it, in order to prepare ourselves even better. But it doesn't matter how well prepared we are. We will depend on the weather and it can neither be predicted nor altered in any way. Once our lines are let go, we will be in a boat 22 feet long with a beam of six feet, without motor or radar, completely and utterly at the mercy of the elements.

Jamie Young, one of the Irishmen who attempted to follow Shackleton's route a few years earlier and who gave up after three 180-degree capsizes, wrote to me:

"My greatest fear was that the boat would be rolled over by a huge sea. That happened. If the weather had gotten worse and the wind had struck me at more than 65 knots, the boat might have come apart at its weakest point in the cock-pit area. If it really gets stormy out there, your support vessel might as well be on the other side of the world. In any bad weather, our support vessel was miles away and struggling to take care of herself. The only means of coming together were radio and GPS. Had either of them broken down, we would still be out there today."

These then are the realities. The DAGMAR AAEN will not be close to us anyway, as the IFAGE camera team wants to call at the South Shetland Islands to do another documentary film about the Antarctic. Actually, one or two rendezvous are planned during the course of the expedition for filming and photographing the JAMES CAIRD II but, apart from that, she will be performing other tasks and give us a wide berth at all times. We will be alone, on the stormiest ocean on the planet.

The guidebook *British Antarctic Pilot* puts our concerns in black and white: 70% of the waves are higher than 12 feet. The highest waves reach 75 feet and, in exceptional in-stances, 105 feet. All year round, the weather is comparable to winter weather in the North Atlantic. The worst conditions are encountered in the region of the South Orkney Islands, where average wind velocities reach gale force (that is, Force 10) 160 days of the year. March, August and September are considered the stormiest, the other months being roughly consistent except that, in winter, it is colder and the days shorter.

Shackleton went through it in the worst weather—why shouldn't we be able to make it?

January 19. We cannot find any more excuses for putting off our departure. It is time to get started. Since yesterday we have been lying alongside the DAGMAR AAEN at anchor—that is, when the anchor holds. One problem when sailing in these waters is the very poor holding quality of the bottom. It doesn't matter where; the slightest gust of wind will make the anchor drag. Not just for us, but for any vessel, big or small. Esperanza Bay is no exception. We spend the last day setting and re-setting the anchor. For the moment it is holding.

We sit comfortably aboard the DAGMAR AAEN for one last time and delight in stuffing ourselves with food. In the days that follow our appetites will decline noticeably. At four p.m. we set sail and cast off the lines. The wind is from the east at Force 4, the sun is shining and the bay practically smooth. Henryk is at the tiller; he tacks, Sigga and I shift the yard of the mainsail and off the JAMES CAIRD II goes, racing seaward. We estimate our speed at a good five knots. By the time DAGMAR AAEN has weighed anchor and can overhaul us under power, we have almost cleared the bay. All four of us are on deck—three can sit in the cockpit while the fourth perches on the deck.

Dead ahead lies glacier-draped Joinville Island, a bit north of which is Bransfield and the mountains of d'Urville Island. As we leave Esperanza Bay behind and enter the Antarctic Sound—the part of the ocean between the islands and the Antarctic Peninsula—the tranquility ends abruptly. Short waves smack against the hull, driving the first spray over the deck. The DAGMAR AAEN, still keeping close to us for filming, pitches only slightly in the seas. What a difference a few extra yards of length make in a boat. We're cold for the first time. Aboard the DAGMAR AAEN before sailing we filled the thermos with hot tea; now, when merely pouring it into the mug, it sloshes all over my gloves. I learn very quickly how complicated even the simplest movement can be. Bracing myself in the companionway and keeping the thermos pinned between my knees, I hold the mug in my left hand and try to screw on the thermos stopper with my right. After a zillion tries, I manage to do it, but half the tea has disappeared from the cup and the rest is now only lukewarm. How can this be happening when, for the moment, the weather is still quite good?

In the interim, DAGMAR AAEN has deserted us. After the camera crew finishes filming our departure, Karsten sets sail and makes for Deception Island. Among the icebergs, the North Sea cutter looks like a plaything. How minuscule we must look. We still have a favoring wind, but it is slackening. Our first night at sea has begun. The ocean is getting rough; every now and then icy seawater smacks us in the face. We're on our way!

Sea watches commence right from the start. I'm on watch from midnight to 3 a.m. I will be relieved by Martin who is on deck from 3 a.m. to 6 a.m. During his watch, I am the stand-by, meaning that I sit below decks, fully dressed, ready in the event I am called on deck for any sail handling. In addition, the stand-by must try to do the following: navigate and plot our position on the chart; make entries in the logbook; keep boiling water in order to fill the thermos; provide the helmsman with hot drinks and energy bars; and keep himself fairly warm. The latter task is a total impossibility.

Other tasks are also incredibly demanding, draining our strength. In the preliminary stages, for example, we had intended to keep logs recording our truest, most personal impressions to be able later to get a complete picture. But the mere act of holding a pen in wet, cold hands and of trying to keep the paper dry, turns out to be too hard, so the idea is soon discarded. The constant rolling and pitching does not exactly promote concentration—at least, not the kind that would be required to produce any sort of readable sentences. Thus for our remembrances we must rely on a few brief notes.

Relief comes only after the stand-by watch. Martin is relieved by Sigga and he, in turn, goes on stand-by, until finally Henryk takes over from Sigga, whom I again will relieve at 12 noon. The system proves efficient. We can't expect anyone to stay on deck for more than three hours straight. No matter how many layers of fleece you put on, after three hours in this kind of weather, you are frozen through and through.

In that span of time, the concentration essential for safe sailing diminishes dangerously. And the watch below can bring little in the way of assistance. The temperature down there reaches the level of the ocean water temperature, so your stand-by is already at the freezing point. Add to this the dampness inside the boat—sogginess is the more accurate term. The deck is like a dripstone cave, in which moisture condenses as drops of water. With our breath, our sodden clothes, the steam created by boiling water—the boat never feels dry.

There is also the fact that our two flexible water tanks abruptly decided to leak, emptying their contents into the boat. We have a small bilge pump but, with all the pitching and tossing, we simply cannot get all the water over the side. The leaking tanks cause us some concern, not only because our water supply has dwindled appreciably. Much worse, the weight of the water plays an important role in calculating our ballast. How will those missing four hundred pounds make themselves felt? How will we be affected by the lack of water? We anticipated breakdowns, but a problem of this magnitude right at the outset may jeopardize the whole voyage.

The only place where you can sit without having to pin your chin on your breastbone is the head. Ours consists of a galvanized iron pail placed right under the companionway. When this makeshift toilet is not in use, its wooden cover serves as a seat for the stand-by. A good feature of that spot is that we can wedge our bodies between the two handrails and we have our hands free. We need them to light the Primus stove that's built into an odd-looking contraption designed by Henryk under our mini-table.

Stowed there, the pressure cooker is safe. "Pressure cooker" suggests that we do some serious cooking, which is anything but the case. We opted for the cooker solely because the lid could be sealed and, hence, was leak-proof, a safety feature to protect us from being scalded with boiling water. But the essential prerequisite for a boat journey of this kind is a cast-iron stomach. On deck, things may not be too awfully bad; below decks we need nerves of steel. A stale, fetid odor emanates from wet socks, seawater, morsels of food and, occasionally, from the head—and, sadly, little can be done about it. Under the floorboards, bilgewater sloshes back and forth, cake crumbs mingling with scraps of paper. Finally, down below, the very motion of the boat is enough to turn our stomachs.

After we have survived the three hours on watch, it's then time for undressing: seaboots, oilskins, watch caps, gloves, various fleece layers and underwear. The rude awakening comes later, when the next watch comes on. All that clothing manages to wind up—less than neatly—in some corner, without the slightest possibility of ever drying out there. For the moment, this hardly matters to us. What counts right now is the sleeping bag, our best friend on the whole voyage.

We opted for the "Sastrugi" model from Jack Wolfskin, the warmest sleeping bag I know. Thus far we have used them only on wintry polar expeditions. They provide comfortable sleeping at temperatures up to −40 degrees Celsius. A few people sniggered when we chose a bag rated for this temperature, "After all, you aren't getting any younger," but it is perfect for our purposes. After a total of six hours on watch we are so frozen stiff that only the warmest bag is warm enough.

At the same time our sleeping areas—I can't bring myself to term these claustrophobic shelves *bunks*—represent the only place aboard where we can stretch out, rather than constantly being in some uncomfortable squatting, kneeling or sitting position. Within half an hour we feel the warmth slowly going through our bodies. For some obscure reason, though, it stops knee-high. Our legs and feet stay cold throughout the entire journey. It's not the fault of our equipment, certainly not the specially designed seaboots; rather, with all the crouching we suffer from poor circulation. But, clearly, the sleeping bag is the sweetest place on board.

Because of our large frames, Martin and I get the *deluxe* bunks up forward, about which we are both quite happy. Sigga and Henryk, somewhat smaller than either of us, take the quarter berths to port and starboard of the cockpit. These sleeping niches are not only exceedingly narrow, but whenever somebody climbs through the companionway, the sleeper may get a shower. The direct proximity of the head might also be considered something of a drawback. The potential user discreetly unrolls a flap of canvas on either side of the head to assure a modicum of privacy. But the faces of the two miserable sleepers are mere inches from—*the happening.* When we *sit,* we are on full display. But we simply can't afford daintiness on this boat.

Wind and weather change constantly. At times we lie totally becalmed in a choppy sea, trying desperately to dodge icebergs. The conditions of the current are a problem for any boat the size of JAMES CAIRD II. All too closely we pass some icebergs from which back eddies are clearly visible. Just when we get past one of these white giants, the current seizes us, driving the boat back toward the berg. We constantly take bearings, concerned about which side we should pass the iceberg on and about which way the current is setting us. But it wouldn't require an iceberg to sink our boat. Her planking is just three-quarters of an inch thick, with no additional sheathing for the ice. One odd growler—and there are thousands of these—would be all it would take when we're moving along at a fast pace. Drifting without wind among these bergs is particularly unpleasant. We are pleased when, in the course of the day, a fresh breeze pipes up again—too bad it's blowing from almost dead ahead. We must tack.

Boats like the JAMES CAIRD II were originally designed as lifeboats—not sailboats. Accordingly, she has little windward ability. Depending on wind and waves, we can point up about 70 degrees to the wind. But she makes a great deal of leeway. Tacking with the CAIRD II is not particularly conducive to sailing enjoyment. The bow smacks into the seas with a bang, the helmsman is literally drenched and even the close-hauled mizzen doesn't make our position more comfortable belowdeck. Sleep? Forget that idea. For a fraction of a second you're glued to the underside of the deck, then you drop back down—fortunately, only about 14 inches separate deck from bunk. To us, it feels like riding a Brahma bull permanently. "The body needs time to get used to the frantic motion of the boat," we tell ourselves. But after three days things don't get better—they only get worse.

The weather is doing its best to ruin this adventure for us. We are only at the start and it literally makes us puke. The worst part is being cold and wet. Since arriving in Bransfield Strait, the swells have taken on very different dimensions. Now there's a certain purposefulness about the individual seas. Off our port side we take a bearing on tiny, volcanic Bridgeman Island. For the first time we can make out the outline of Clarence and Elephant islands in the distance. But we cannot steer for either island. Another one appears dead ahead—Gibbs Island. Thilo Natke had told us something about a sheltered bay there—at least, the prospect of one. Light-years seem to separate us from the cozy atmosphere of the HANSEATIC but actually it was just a week ago that he gave me this valuable tip.

For Sigga, the change from a life of luxury and idleness aboard the HANSEATIC to the Spartan conditions of the JAMES CAIRD II is perfectly logical: "I see the voyage as a challenge, one that involves both coexisting on board as well as struggling with nature. Here we live so intensely. Most people live alone—and that isn't living."

Who would have dreamt that the most difficult aspects of a journey like this would be to change our clothes and the business of going to the head? On the HANSEATIC we certainly never gave such matters a second thought.

On January 22 heavy clouds and mist rob us of any real visibility. After we have Gibbs Island off our starboard bow, the wind shifts again. We will make the island by steering 68 degrees over the ground—that is, if we can hold this heading. We make a series of long tacks until the snow- and ice-draped summit of the island looms ahead. With the barometric pressure falling and the weather visibly deteriorating, we decide to put into "Thilo's Bay," as we have now named it.

7

In the Grip of Antarctica

Dozens of stranded icebergs crowd the entrance to "Thilo's Bay" and act as a breakwater. The wind blows down from the mountains right into our face. Skillfully, Martin makes a series of short tacks to get us past the bergs and into the bay. Once inside, we are becalmed so that the sails, suddenly useless, hang down like bags. It is time to row. We get the oars out and Henryk and I begin struggling with the unwieldy things. We move ahead very slowly but, at least, it's in the right direction. How quickly we learn to appreciate the smallest favors! When there is even a slight ground swell, the oars can become useless and even dangerous. There just isn't enough room in the tiny cockpit for us to put all our muscle into the oars. For the moment, however, they stand us in good stead.

The stench from the penguin colony on the cliffs assails our nostrils. The clamor made by thousands of these creatures attending to their brooding—at times, quite high up on vertical walls—is positively deafening. Waddling, sliding, they descend from rocks and snow stained red with their guano, to go plunging headlong into the surf. There, in what is essentially their element, the penguins quickly resurface, preening and cleaning their travel-soiled plumage before departing, in small bands, to hunt for krill or octopus. The little chicks look very well-nourished, suggesting that there is plenty to eat here. A few fur seals wallow and roll on the beach. These creatures can be very quarrelsome and pugnacious. At times their fearsome clashes result in the loser dying of his wounds. They are as unfriendly and aggressive to humans as to their own kind.

We never cease to be amazed at how ready the fur seals are to sprint after someone with the unmistakable aim of biting him. Their bite being as dangerous as that of any beast of prey, we firmly resolve to keep a civil distance at all times. No way will we get chummy with fur seals. Like the far larger sea elephants, the fur seals were nearly exterminated in the days of sealing and whaling. At the time of the ENDURANCE expedition, most Antarctic beaches had been swept clean and depopulated. So thoroughly did the seal-hunters do their work that, at times, it was feared that the whole species was extinct. Those fears were not far from wrong. Whaling continued in these waters until the 1960s when the last whaling station on South Georgia closed down. Seal hunting, on the other hand, had been abandoned in the previous decade, there being simply no seals left by then. Today the seals have returned to their old breeding grounds and, in some areas, their numbers are growing prodigiously.

We look for a place on the beach where none of these creatures can be spotted. While Sigga and Martin furl the sails, Henryk and I row deeper into the bay. Then, in fifteen feet of water, we anchor, paying out the rode carefully. Almost too good to be true, the anchor seems to be holding. We start breathing again. The sudden tranquility that reigns on board is overwhelming. The boat is rolling very gently in the slight swell running in the bay, but for us it's almost a lullabye. We are dead-tired. The only one of its kind, this bay provides shelter from the deteriorating weather.

All of a sudden we hear a loud growling. A sea lion we missed? Not at all—it's our stomachs rumbling. Astonished, we realize that we have hardly eaten a thing in the last few days. Now the hunger pangs are making themselves felt.

We open the hatch to let some air into our dripstone cave. Sigga lights the Primus stove. First, there's tea and coffee; afterwards, we will consume huge portions of chili con carne. At least, we think we will. The deck is cluttered with the anchor rode, sheets and halyards, the lowered yard. We'll clear that raffle in a minute but, right now, food and drink are more important. Big mistake.

Is it because of our fatigue that we fail to size up the ominous weather or are we simply careless? Looking back, I simply can't explain it. The squall draws closer, its strength increasing and, suddenly, we are being pushed into the middle of the bay. We're dragging our anchor.

Now, because of our totally unseamanlike behavior, everything has to go like clockwork. The wind is driving us toward the cliffs on the other side of the bay. We already hear the thundering breakers there. We attempt to row and soon realize that we haven't a hope against wind and waves. The boat is too heavy and too cramped for us to pull the oars properly. So we make sail, but that's easier said than done. In the raffle of running rigging, it's almost impossible to lay our hands on the right sheet or right halyard. The cliffs now loom threateningly close. On the pitching, rolling deck, I somehow manage to get the anchor in and set the jib while Martin and Henryk struggle with the main.

Poor Sigga, belowdeck, tries grimly to keep the contents of the pots from spilling. Somehow, we manage to set all sail though the mess is indescribable. We barely have steerage-way. As the icebergs steal our wind, we have trouble coming about. In short, choppy seas, the bow refuses to go through the eye of the wind. To change tacks, we are forced to gybe her around. This involves a certain amount of danger, takes time and loses us hard-won ground. But we have no other choice. Slowly, frighteningly close to the cliffs and icebergs, we manage to sail out of the bay.

Once outside we receive the full brunt of wind and sea. In minutes, we are drenched. Vainly, we attempt to beat back into the bay. We make absolutely no headway against wind and waves. Finally, when the deck is shipshape once more, we change course.

It will take us 14 hours to regain the bay. Fourteen miserable hours during which each of us is privately wondering why we're doing what we're doing. At the same time, our thoughts return to the past. What if the going gets rough? After all, we're only risking our own fool necks. For Shackleton, however, the added physical and mental pressure that those 27 lives must have represented is almost unimaginable. We gain new respect for his achievement.

When, exhausted, we regain the head of the bay, Henryk, wearing his survival suit, jumps off the bow into the surf and makes our long rode fast to a huge rock. We put our anchor over the stern to prevent the boat from yawing. This time, it holds. Our chili con carne is still congealing on the floorboards, sluicing around in bilgewater, refuse and hair. We lose our appetites and dump the contents of the pot overboard. We only want to sleep. For the first time, we get our little kerosene heater going. Owing to space limitations, it is so minuscule that its reason for being is more psychological than practical. All the same, we delight in each added degree of temperature. We take turns standing anchor watch, while the others fall into a deep slumber. We continue, in shifts, until everyone feels fit and rested again. Only then do we total up the score.

Henryk minces no words in expressing what we all think about the clutter on deck: "That deck looked like a damned shithouse. I figure we have a hundred years' sea-time all combined, and none of us has ever been through chaos like that before. We should all be ashamed of ourselves."

Since our departure from Esperanza, we have made 130 nautical miles as the crow flies; actually, with all the tacking we have come much further than that. A normal cruising sailboat could cover this kind of distance in one day.

When people speak of the ENDURANCE expedition, they generally refer only to the boat journey from Elephant Island to South Georgia. Certainly, that leg is the longest and, as concerns rough seas, the most exposed. But this is misleading. Bransfield Strait is some 60 miles wide and completely exposed. Gibbs, Elephant and Clarence islands lie distinctly to the north and thus are squarely in the area of the Drake Passage. That means storm-swept seas. Relatively low temperatures as well as ice and strong currents compound the problem on this stretch. Also, the wind and waves change all the time. It is unfair to belittle that first phase of the journey, as was the case in the two earlier attempts to reconstruct Shackleton's journey.

When Shackleton and his crew left their eroding ice floe and took to the lifeboats on April 9, 1916, their position was 61 degrees 56 minutes south and 053 degrees 56 minutes west. From this point to Cape Valentine, where they first landed on Elephant Island, there are only 54 nautical miles, a trifling distance when measured on the chart. Yet it took them a week to complete this leg. While they were headed for King George Island with a fair east wind, they encountered a strong surface current which set them over 20 miles to the southeast—precisely in the opposite direction. This knowledge must have been a crushing blow to the exhausted men.

Shackleton changed course and now tried to reach Esperanza but the wind promptly veered to the southeast, so they had to change course and were finally pushed towards Elephant Island. The island was by then about 100 miles away. The currents and winds had played a cruel game with the men. It must have been these experiences that finally prompted Shackleton to embark on the journey to South Georgia in just one boat, thereby running enormous risks. Otherwise his decision becomes very hard for me to understand. In his day, presumably, neither Elephant nor Clarence islands had been explored. At least, there was no information available about them. On the other hand, King George Island and the islands that stretch in a southwesterly direction had not only been charted and routinely visited by whalers and seal-hunters, but reports showed that a sheltered bay existed there. In addition, the terrain is relatively flat. In Deception Island's crater, accessible from the sea, there were food depots and buildings—even a little chapel built by the whalers. Knowing all this, Shackleton had originally meant to sail there. Whether he knew anything about the bay we visited on Gibbs Island seems unlikely, however. Together with Clarence and Elephant islands, Gibbs acts as an impassable bulwark, but it offers more shelter than any spot on Elephant Island. He didn't know that, but the island was on the charts and the distance to it comparatively short.

The dangers involved in a boat journey of this kind must have been so frightening to the castaways that, quite sensibly, they rejected any notion of making a further try for King George Island. If necessary McNeish, the capable ship's carpenter, could probably have built a larger boat out of the wooden buildings there. There was every reason to believe that, instead of sailing for South Georgia, they could have hopped from Gibbs to King George Island, even after landing on Elephant Island. Now, in virtually the opposite direction, we will be making the leg from Gibbs Island to Point Wild.

On January 25, the DAGMAR AAEN enters the bay. Besides anchoring over the bow, Karsten and his crew send a long line ashore from the stern, making it fast to a rock there. A good move. In the interim the weather has deteriorated, ruling out any thought of pushing on. A fierce squall interspersed with snow and hail swoops down from the mountains and, outside, rough seas have built up. While the bay may not be very cozy, it is relatively safe and that, basically, is what counts.

The bad weather lasts until January 27. That day at noon the wind abruptly drops off. The sun burns through and suddenly the world looks friendly again. At times during the storm we felt like we were on another planet. That same afternoon we make sail. The DAGMAR AAEN circles us a few times for the benefit of the cameras and then bears off for Elephant Island. She is long gone while we struggle to round Cape Plenty in big seas and little wind.

At 2200 hours we lie totally becalmed halfway between Gibbs and Elephant islands, which looms clearly dead ahead. From Cape Plenty on Gibbs to Cape Lookout on Elephant Island is a mere 15 nautical miles. Cape Lookout offers by far the best landing possibilities on the whole island, something we were able to see for ourselves on the trip there with the HANSEATIC. This time, we dispense with a landing. We make only pitiful headway and not until noon on the 28 do we come abeam the heights of Endurance Glacier, in an ocean so flat and calm that even the tiny JAMES CAIRD II sits there motionless. That's Antarctic weather, too.

We cannot round Cape Valentine until ten o'clock the next morning. Then we clearly see the place where they beached the three lifeboats in 1916. The beach strewn with shingle, the craggy rock faces, the cliffs rising offshore—those who dared to land here had to be utterly desperate. We make no attempt to emulate them. Though the sea is still quite calm, breakers are crashing on the beach. The JAMES CAIRD II is far too heavy for the four of us to haul ashore or to keep off the menacing rocks. Shackleton had 28 men at his disposal, but even they would have unloaded the heavy JAMES CAIRD before beaching her. So we continue on our way down the coast.

Above us loom bleak mountains covered with ice and snow. Somewhat more distant Clarence Island resembles a gigantic block of ice, its sides probably so steep that even the seals and penguins can find no foothold. The crew of the

DAGMAR AAEN intends to visit the island somewhat later. First, however, we make plans for the two vessels to rendezvous off Point Wild to film the old campsite of the castaways. It is about seven miles from Cape Valentine to Point Wild with no possibility of landing in between.

I can imagine how those men felt when, after barely a day on solid earth, Shackleton ordered them back out in a lifeboat. Their mission: scout for a campsite safer than the one at Cape Valentine. One night's rest on that stony beach could scarcely have permitted them to regain their strength. The boat's party must have been in mortal dread of becoming separated from their comrades, for any sudden deterioration in the weather and the impossibility of landing anywhere meant being blown out to sea. Could men in their condition have managed to beat back against the wind to Elephant Island? They must have hugged that coast for fear of being driven into the open ocean. This would seem to explain why they chose Point Wild so quickly. Their fears were after all well founded: just after the castaways found the new site and set up a temporary camp, a fierce gale hit them. During that four-day blow, an incredibly strong gust picked up one of their beached boats like a toy and spun it around.

In sunny weather, we rendezvous off Point Wild. It is our tenth day since setting out from Hope Bay.

8

Achieving the Impossible

Shackleton wrote that the new site was "by no means an ideal camping ground; it was rough, bleak and inhospitable." Actually, his comment can be ascribed to the British penchant for understatement. Even in the fine, sunny weather we are enjoying, it is evident that the bay must have seemed bleak and unfriendly to a castaway. Indeed Frank Hurley, the expedition photographer, described the coast as "dark and foreboding."

The head of the bay is choked with ice from a glacier whose constant rumblings and deafening crashes signal the calving of new bergs. For the unhurried observer, the whole thing represents a powerful sight. Given their situation, however, the crew of the ENDURANCE could scarcely have appreciated the beauty of nature.

It is no easy matter for the DAGMAR AAEN to find an anchorage, as the water is deep and offers poor holding ground. It is only in this calm and sunny weather that we can anchor here. I still remember exactly how the bay appeared from the HANSEATIC. That day, it looked the way it must have looked to Shackleton; staying there for any length of time was out of the question for us. Probably, back in 1915, the glacier jutted out even further into the bay than it does today. That could scarcely have given the castaways any more shelter. The rocky spit, on which their camp was established, is about 180 yards long and 30 yards wide. Fingerlike, it extends seaward and ends in a flat rock forming a kind of breakwater. The cape is named Point Wild, either after Frank Wild or because the seas batter it with such violence. The spit of land abuts a sheer rock wall. There is neither a cave nor a boulder behind which one might seek shelter from storm and cold. To make matters worse, the camp site lies only a few yards above the high-water mark, so there must have been days when heavy seas rolled across this pebbled spit of land.

Even in the placid sea we have today, the DAGMAR AAEN's rubber dinghy is shipping water over its gunwales as we approach. The cliffs and crags, which appear in Hurley's old photographs, remain unchanged since those days, as if time had stood still. Approaching this spot gives us a strange feeling. Cautiously, we go around the submerged rocks. One last breaker pushes us to the little gravel beach and then we are up to our ankles in slimy, reddish penguin guano. Point Wild is not uninhabited: the penguins are standing, packed together; among them lie fur seals lifting their heads aggressively while giving indignant snorts. The place stinks to high heaven and it finally dawns on me what Shackleton meant when he wrote afterwards that the body heat of the men in their sleeping bags melted not only the snow and ice but also the penguin droppings that permeated their clothing and equipment. It takes just one whiff of such a penguin rookery to understand his comment.

Cautiously, so as not to disturb any of the wildlife, we climb over the rocks to the cliffs and walk a few steps to a bronze bust that stands on a rusting pedestal. The bust was erected by the Chileans a few years ago—not to the memory of Shackleton's men—but, rather, to Captain Pardo, the Chilean who, on instructions from Shackleton and Worsley, finally recovered the marooned sailors with his small tug YELCHO. Starkly contrasting with the landscape, the bust seems as incongruous here as a penguin in a big city thoroughfare.

The penguins themselves seem quite unperturbed. Sheltered in the lee of the statue, a small gentoo penguin is taking great pains to hatch an egg. Magnificent, well-fed chicks already sit in all the other nests. It is very late in the season, so this penguin has little hope of raising its offspring. Ten years ago at Terra Nova Bay in the Ross Sea, I had the opportunity to visit an Adelie penguin rookery. As it was already late in the year, all the parents had long since departed with their "seaworthy" broods. Remaining were only the young not sturdy enough to set out on the long journey. The scene was terrible. Skua gulls, those great birds of prey, swooped around, killing one chick after another. Generally, the skuas tore open the chick's belly with their beaks, devoured a little of its insides and then headed for the next victim. I will never forget the sight of all those dying and dead penguin chicks. A similar fate is doubtless awaiting this unhatched chick.

Before we left Germany, Torsten had Frank Hurley's photographs enlarged and brought them to Antarctica. Using these prints, we can orient ourselves easily. We see the knoll where the marooned sailors planned to light a beacon fire if they sighted a passing ship. Exploring the cliffs, the camp-site—Hurley's photographs make it all quite simple. The Irish expedition that worked here in 1997 even brought a metal detector to hunt for any hidden pieces of equipment. After all, the men of the ENDURANCE lived here for over four months. Two of their lifeboats, along with all of their gear, were left behind on the spit of land. So the possibility of finding something, even after such a passage of time, was quite real. But the Irish researchers uncovered nothing. The site looked barren and, actually, it is just that. When, only a few years after the disastrous voyage, Frank Wild returned to Point Wild with the QUEST expedition, he was unable to land; even from his ship he couldn't find out what had become of the remains of the lifeboats. Storms had swept all trace of them into the sea.

But let us glance back at the past. On April 20, 1915, Shackleton informed the men that he intended to sail to South Georgia with only one lifeboat and a small crew. On reaching that island, he would organize a rescue effort from the whaling station there. The ship's carpenter, McNeish, was assigned the task of strengthening their largest, sturdiest boat, the JAMES CAIRD, as much as possible. Though having only a few hand tools and almost no materials at his disposal, he had already repaired the boats two or three times while they were drifting on the ice. The 57-year-old McNeish worked untiringly on the boat in the worst kind of weather. That makes it hard to understand why Shackleton considered him a chronic troublemaker. Couldn't he have praised the carpenter's work and, perhaps, in this way, softened the man's disposition?

McNeish stiffened the JAMES CAIRD by bolting the DUDLEY DOCKER's mast to her keelson. He had already raised the DUDLEY DOCKER's sides during the period on the ice; now he salvaged that planking so he could give the JAMES CAIRD a flush deck from stem to stern. He made deck beams out of sled runners and onto this framework nailed the lids of packing crates. Finally, he stretched sailcloth over the decking to make it watertight.

All available men were put to work on preparations for the great voyage. Those not directly engaged in boat joinery worked at filling bags with sand and round stones as ballast, sorting equipment or completing the camp where those remaining behind would have to survive the winter storms. Several of the men got frostbitten hands merely performing these tasks in wet, freezing conditions.

The provisions stowed aboard the JAMES CAIRD included three cases of sledging ration, two cases of nut food, bouillon cubes, powdered milk, ship's biscuits, sugar and salt. They also took around twenty gallons of kerosene and two Primus stoves with a complete set of spare parts. For each man in the boat's party there was a reindeer-skin sleeping bag.

Being the most experienced navigator, Worsley was assigned the difficult task of guiding the 22-foot boat to its landfall. In addition to a sextant, he carried his chronometer on a lanyard around his neck, something that must have been awkward when determining longitude. Worsley also brought the required navigational tables, a compass, charts and a pair of binoculars. The boat's equipment consisted of four oars, a bilge pump, a drum of oil, an oil bag for spreading oil on the water in a storm, a sea anchor with a long line; one medicine chest, a shotgun with ammunition, as well as fishing gear, candles and matches. The JAMES CAIRD carried two casks of fresh water each containing about 35 gallons.

On April 24 they launched the boat and then set about loading her with ballast and stores. The boat was low in the water—too low in Worsley's opinion. But Shackleton feared that, with less ballast, she might capsize easily. The heavy boat would certainly be more stable though, presumably, she would be slower and would sail a good deal wetter. Outside the breakers, the fully laden JAMES CAIRD lay at anchor with a bow line ashore. Aside from Shackleton and Worsley, Crean, McNeish, McCarthy and Vincent would be making the trip. Shackleton placed Frank Wild, his closest friend and confidant, in charge of the men he was leaving behind. He knew all too well that strong leadership was needed to bring the men safely through the winter with its anticipated privations and monotony. Other than himself he trusted only Frank Wild with this task.

At noon the boat was ready to sail. After Shackleton had delegated all the necessary authority to his friend Wild, the men bid each other farewell and, minutes later, the JAMES CAIRD set sail. It was not long before the boat was headed in a northerly direction toward a more than uncertain fate.

It is difficult to accept the decision to take a boat as small as the JAMES CAIRD to South Georgia without wondering if there were not viable alternatives, or why Shackleton opted for the longest and, presumably, the most dangerous of all routes. The following possibilities need to be discussed.

1. They were about 500 nautical miles from Cape Horn, or the South American continent;

2. the Falkland Islands were some 550 miles off;

3. the distance to South Georgia was approximately 700 miles;

4. King George and Deception islands presented an alternative.

Cape Horn had to be eliminated because of the prevailing currents and unfavorable winds anticipated. Shackleton had originally favored the idea of making the journey via Drake Passage, but Worsley convinced him that it couldn't be done in a boat like the CAIRD.

The Falklands would certainly have been an alternative to South Georgia but Shackleton decided against them, too, fearing unfavorable winds and currents. Why he failed to choose the fourth possibility can only be explained by the desperate plight of his men. It is a good 100 nautical miles from Cape Valentine to King George. They could have sailed 20 miles of that distance in the shelter of Elephant Island's coast and, at the same time, have found a far better campsite at Cape Lookout. The distance from Cape Lookout to Gibbs Island—with its "Thilo's Bay"—was 15 miles and from Gibbs to King George less than 70 miles. From there on, they would have had the protection of a relatively accessible coast with a number of landing places and, considering the weather conditions, could have reached Deception Island. There, they would have been safe for the time being—that much was certain—even if they'd had to wait longer for rescue.

However, the chances of reaching South Georgia in a boat like the JAMES CAIRD were minute. And that's why Shackleton's decision not to consider the latter route is so hard for me to fathom.

With all due respect for the men's endurance, for Shackleton's leadership ability, and for Worsley's navigation and seamanship, they needed a lot of luck to go where they finally went. Lady Luck can't be ordered up on demand—she's just there or she isn't. But luck was the measure of all things for making a successful passage. Their decision to rule out Deception Island can only be explained by the morale factor and that some men were in poor health. Certainly, in his heart of hearts, Shackleton must have considered the option. It might also have been the psychological aspect that this route held for him: Deception Island meant sailing back into the Antarctic, instead of going north.

In a very direct way, even we—who merely re-enact their adventure—go through the anxieties and fears associated with the rescue mission to South Georgia. The very audacity of their decision nearly drains us of all our energy. Had the JAMES CAIRD failed to make South Georgia, no help would have arrived for the men at Point Wild—condemning them to a lingering death. As Shackleton himself told Worsley on the journey: "Skipper, if anything should happen to me while those fellows are waiting for me, I shall feel like a murderer." Better than anyone else, Shackleton and Worsley knew just how risky their venture was.

While the weather in this part of the world may be unpredictable and stormy, there are always intervals of fair weather, something that holds true in both summer and winter. In the lifeboats, the men could have done the relatively short leg in the direction of King George Island in one day. They had after all picked their weather or could have waited for better conditions. At any rate, during the entire journey

Sir Ernest Shackleton.
I spent over ten years thinking
about the man and his voyage
before I dared to embark on our
adventure aboard JAMES CAIRD II.
*Scott Polar Research Institute,
Cambridge, United Kingdom*

On the way to the
Antarctic Peninsula, the
entrance to Le Maire Channel.
Brigitte Ellerbrock

During our crossing of the Antarctic in 1989/90 we visited the Discovery camp set up by Scott. It still contains foodstuffs from Scott's and Shackleton's expeditions. The camp is not far from McMurdo station. *Arved Fuchs*

On December 30, 1989, Reinhold Messner and I reached the South Pole. In the foreground the precise point of the South Pole is clearly marked. The dome in the background contains the living quarters of the American scientists and crews at McMurdo station. *Arved Fuchs*

The beginning of the end. ENDURANCE is locked in the ice of the
Weddell Sea. This photo by Frank Hurley became world famous.
Royal Geographic Society, London

Launch of JAMES CAIRD II, October 2, 1999. In the background, the
DAGMAR AAEN which was overhauled in the same boatyard. Three days
later, she is on her way to Antarctica. *Torsten Heller*

JAMES CAIRD II under construction in Denmark. Our replica is being built following the exact plans and with the same materials as the original JAMES CAIRD. *Torsten Heller*

JAMES CAIRD II is being lowered from the German cruise ship HANSEATIC in Esperanza Bay. Shortly thereafter we are alone and the adventure is about to begin. *Brigitte Ellerbrock*

The nights are bitter cold and pitch-dark. We have to steer with utmost caution to avoid the ice which is everywhere. *Henryk Wolski*

We need to maintain our strength. Despite the rough seas, Sigga and Martin try to prepare some food. *Torsten Heller*

The icebergs in front of Gibbs Island give us some protection.
Like a huge breakwater, they protect the bay from the open sea.
Torsten Heller

We approach Cape Valentine on Elephant Island. It is here that Shackleton's exhausted crew first set foot on land after more than a week in the lifeboats. *Arved Fuchs*

DAGMAR AAEN at Point Wild. Our film crew arrived on this exceptionally calm and beautiful day. *Torsten Heller*

they would never encounter conditions worse than those off Point Wild.

Shackleton decided to go for South Georgia, so we're in for it too. After our excursion on the beach, we top up the water supply of the JAMES CAIRD II and try to relax a bit on board the DAGMAR AAEN. To make sure that we have a peaceful night without the anchor dragging, Karsten puts ashore a line to which we simply secure JAMES CAIRD II. Once more, the four of us sleep under the protection of the DAGMAR AAEN's anchor watch. Then, on the morning of January 30, we transfer over to our big North Sea cutter for the last meal of the condemned. At 1000 hours we let go the lines and row easily out of the bay. Torsten and Ralf accompany us part of the way in the dinghy to photograph and videotape our departure. We set sail. At first, the wind comes from the northeast and then, a bit later, shifts to the east. Accordingly, we can steer 020 degrees—right on our desired course. Cirrus clouds are building in the sky, the first sign of worsening weather. We have to get going—under no circumstances do we want to be lying off Point Wild in heavy weather. We'd sooner ride out any storm in the open sea.

As is often the case, gloomy thoughts are followed by even darker events. We don't have to wait long for the next gale. By 12 noon heavier swells make themselves felt but, for the moment, we do four knots under full sail as the wind is an agreeable Force 4. The barometer is falling steadily. The sky is covered with a milky-white layer of cirrus clouds, the coast of Elephant Island now only visible through a veil of mist. Toward afternoon the wind freshens, the air grows warmer and, as a harbinger of bad weather, the seas run higher and higher.

The weather has also deteriorated for the DAGMAR AAEN and she has left her anchorage. Karsten and his crew head for Clarence Island while we, alone and lonely, sail into the uncertainty of a gale-tossed night on the earth's most inhospitable ocean.

9

Into the Unknown

Towards evening, the weather again worsens, leaving little doubt about who is making the ground rules. The uneasy peace in the past couple of days of sun and calm is definitely over.

Crouching or sitting, we huddle together in utter misery aboard our cockleshell. Showers of hail scour the deck, the barometric pressure has dropped to 970 millibars and the temperature is at freezing. The ocean looks gray and hostile, as if it had just been biding its time until we were far from any shelter to teach us a lesson. The wind is at Force 6-7 and has been for hours, so a high sea is now running.

Our three-hour tricks at the helm seem interminable. At nightfall the darkness puts an end to any visibility. It is as though a bag had been pulled over our heads. Now steering the little double-ender becomes tiring. The helmsman must stay totally focused every second. The darkness is filled with the crashing of breaking seas. Every so often white crests flash by and then an unexpectedly high comber sends us careening forward in a wild rush. It is no longer any fun.

When I relieve Henryk at midnight, it takes me a few minutes to get my bearings before I can take the tiller from him. Just before coming topside, I hook my safety harness into two different points. That belt is our life insurance. Whenever one of us climbs out of the scuttle, our first act is to snap it into the eyebolt provided for that purpose.

With the running sea, we can never let go of the tiller for even a second. The double-ender behaves well in the following seas, but she cannot steer herself. If we take our hand off the tiller and she goes broadside to the seas, we run the risk of broaching to and being rolled over. Henryk does not remove his hand from the tiller until I have positioned myself and am actually steering. After briefing me about the weather and our heading, he crawls carefully to the scuttle and, wet as he is, scrambles below. Now I am alone.

A wave slams broadside into the side of the boat and fills the tiny cockpit. It is like sitting in a bathtub—only the temperature of the water is rather on the cold side. Again and again, showers of hail pelt my face. Hasn't the weather heard that we are still in summer? I have seldom ever felt so cold. Somehow, water always seeps under our foulweather gear. I think I'm properly dressed to come topside but as soon as that first drenching comes, I feel the trickle of icy water between chin and throat; then it runs down to my chest.

Sitting on the port side, my body is wedged against the mizzenmast. With my left hand, I hang onto the rail; with my right, I grasp the tiller. I am almost a prisoner. Even the hot tea that Henryk usually conjures up on his stand-by watch must be forgotten tonight. That mug of hot tea cheers me up on watch. He tops off this delightful ritual with salami or cheese that he sticks on crackers with mustard so that nothing falls off. For us, at the helm, Henryk's night lunch is better than any four-star restaurant. But, tonight, the watchword is grit and sacrifice, growl and go. Please, somebody, let the tea and crackers come back soon.

Toward the end of my watch I am colder than ever. But the wind has slackened somewhat and when Martin relieves me the first grey light of dawn reveals the nightmarish scene of a raging ocean.

Below, I get my first look at the barometer. It is dropping even lower, so this may be just the calm before the storm. It finally hits during Sigga's watch. The barometer sinks to 966 millibars. The wind now freshens and swings 180 degrees from northeast to southwest. The motion of the boat is unbearable. Sleep? Not a chance. We crouch below, in all our foulweather gear, ready to go topside at any moment.

By 11 a.m., the seas have reached gigantic proportions and the wind has freshened once more. We can no longer sail the boat. Henryk, standing stoically at the helm, has weathered a blizzard and looks like a snowman. In different circumstances, it would be funny. But there's nothing funny about the expression on his face. Today is anything but jolly. We must take in the last scrap of sail and then lie to our sea anchor, waiting for better weather. It's a tactic that Shackleton also used.

We inch forward on our bellies over the snow-covered, pitching deck. We will drop main and jib; at the same time, setting the mizzen will help keep our bow up into the wind. It's like trying to untie knots while riding a bucking bronco.

A comber crashes over the deck, washing away some of the snow. The blizzard lasted only a few minutes but a couple of inches of heavy, wet flakes stick to the sails and cordage. We must work with bare hands, our fingers are stiff with cold and pain. Finally, we get the main yard down and lashed to the deck.

Meanwhile, Sigga is below getting out the sea anchor. It looks like a parachute with a canopy nine feet in diameter. A red buoy serves to keep it at a depth of about six feet and its 450-foot rode is made fast to our stemhead. This will hold the bow of the JAMES CAIRD II into wind and waves, while slowing our drift considerably. The pull exerted by such a drogue is enormous. The length of the rode must be geared to wave height: the longer the rode, the more effective the drogue. As soon as we get parachute and buoy over the side, the line goes whizzing through my hands. I quickly take a turn around the cleat on the forward deck and begin paying out line. Almost immediately, the bow comes up into the wind and our motion becomes easier, slower. In the meanwhile, Henryk lashes the tiller and everything else not actually riveted or nailed down. Now there is nothing left to do topside.

While the seas build ever higher, we crawl below, one after the other, and start pulling off our sodden oilskins. The watchstander sits in the companionway, peeking out occasionally.

The gale hits Force 10 winds, while the spray is driven horizontally and breaking waves rumble ever louder, threatening to engulf JAMES CAIRD II. To us, huddled below, it sounds like someone beating on an empty steel drum with a club. Seas crash over the boat but somehow, amazingly, without doing any real damage. At times, she heels way over but never to the point where we fear she will capsize. I keep thinking of those Irish fellows who survived three 180-degree rolls, each time being half-swamped. Turning three such somersaults completely unnerved them and, understandably, they asked to be taken off by their support vessel. The mental strain had to have been enormous. Why their boat capsized three times I will never know.

Despite her lively motion, JAMES CAIRD II, as close to the original as possible in terms of hull design and construction, inspires confidence and gives a feeling of security. Helmut Radebold, the naval architect responsible for the theoretical and scientific aspects of the project, said that the original boat had proved herself in every respect. It was therefore important that we respect the length and beam of the original, the form of her ribs and, equally, the way in which she was built.

Even the ballasting seems just right—in spite of those leaking water tanks that gave us such a headache at the beginning. At the same time, the boat is so small that she offers breaking seas no serious resistance. Resilient as a cork, she is safe. The bigger the vessel, the more resistance offered to oncoming seas; the impact of the wave becomes that much greater. It is not rare that container ships have their deck loads ripped clean off or their superstructure bashed in. Built as a lifeboat and as uncomfortable and lively as her motion may be, JAMES CAIRD II has a good grip on the weather. Yes, stormy seas may make her shudder and roll her but, for the most part, they simply wash right over her, as if she hardly interests them.

Down below, the acceleration forces are so great, so

unpredictable that, even lying down, triced up in our bunks, we're flung back and forth. My head, in particular, bounces around, so I get no sleep. Any routine chore, any trivial job requires a tremendous show of will power. The absolute worst are the calls of nature. We put off these moments as long as possible, drinking and eating very little, fearful of our next trip to the bucket.

The gale lasts the entire day and the following night. It slowly abates the next morning. At 9 o'clock we carefully begin hauling in the sea anchor. I am amazed at how easy it is to pull in. The mystery is explained when the parachute finally comes into the cockpit. It has been torn to shreds and its drag thereby considerably reduced. Nonetheless, just this resistance—as well as the weight of the long rode—have kept our bow up into the wind.

After the jib, the main is set—we'd left the mizzen up—and then we steer 030 degrees. The wind keeps on dropping, but waves seem to be coming from every which way; we slat around in a kind of corkscrew motion, without knowing whether we're coming or going. The world looks friendlier all the same. From time to time, the cloud cover pulls aside, revealing a little patch of blue sky and even the odd sun ray gets through. That puts some life back into us; when I take the tiller, I relish doing it. Somehow, we feel stronger for having been through that gale. The JAMES CAIRD II has shown her mettle and, what's more, never once made us feel she'd reached her limits. The boat may be terribly uncomfortable to sail, but she's safe.

Since leaving Elephant Island we have kept on as northerly a course as possible. Shackleton had also urged Worsley to sail north as far as possible and not make directly for South Georgia. The experience of the Irish expedition bore out the wisdom of his strategy. Instead of choosing the uncomfortable upwind course, they gave in to the temptation of sailing a downwind course with the hope that the wind would shift later on. In that way, the Irish party came within 20 miles of the South Orkney Islands. According to the Antarctic coast pilot, this group of islands has particularly bad weather, even by local standards, and dangerous cross seas. This is the part of the ocean where the Irish group had their capsizes. We follow Shackleton's sailing instructions to the letter and come out the better for it. Our journey becomes longer, but the direct route is not always the best.

The third night on the ocean since leaving Elephant Island is quiet and lovely. Once more, Henryk provides me with hot tea, crackers with cheese and sausage; he breaks off pieces of Power Bars and BP5. In the past two days, we have eaten next to nothing—now I am getting hunger pangs. For a long time the sky has been full of stars. Henryk is overjoyed. The constellations are clearly visible—even Orion from northern starlit skies. This prompts Henryk to make an enthusiastic entry in the log, "Beautiful, silent night, starry skies. Orion turned upside down and Sirius visible. Is it possible? It makes me feel right at home."

The crew of the DAGMAR AAEN has also felt the storm's impact. After leaving Elephant Island, they headed for Clarence Island to attempt a landing there. Apparently, there was only one possibility of getting ashore, but even that had to be ruled out on account of the weather. The log of the DAGMAR AAEN records wind velocities up to 50 knots, or Force 10. Anchoring off the island was impossible. Even the use of the dinghy to make a landing was too dangerous because of the squalls. Karsten therefore gave up on the idea and ran under jib alone. An attempt to land at Cape Lookout on Elephant Island was also aborted owing to the weather. Instead, they worked at clearing snow off the deck with their shovels. Like us, they decided to lie hove-to, waiting for better weather.

This merely confirms what Jamie Young, a member of the Irish expedition, had said. "When the going gets rough, the support vessel might as well be on the North Sea. In a gale, they'll have their hands full just taking care of themselves." How right he is!

For the first time, Sigga and Martin start cooking. Whenever the lid is removed from the saucepan, the interior of the JAMES CAIRD II fills with thick clouds of steam. A minute later, drops of water begin plopping on to my face, as the steam condenses on the underside of the deck and cools back down. In spite of this, the smell of the food makes our mouths water. We wolf down the delicious stew—so hot that it nearly burns our tongues. It tastes delicious. Things start looking up. In a matter of minutes, we feel the situation isn't all that bad.

Towards evening, the feeling of normalcy is somewhat tempered as the weather again begins deteriorating. We point as high into the wind as we can, shipping water constantly. The hull smacks into the seas and the helmsman spends a couple of hours under a cold shower. When I relieve Henryk at midnight, it is blowing full force again. The ride through total darkness takes our breath away. Like the day before, I get a roller coaster ride that won't end. Unable to react in time to breaking seas that I simply cannot see in the dark, I decide to heave to. With Henryk's help, I get the mainsail in, back the jib and lash the tiller. At once, calm reigns aboard ship—if the term applies to a craft this size. Our feeling of relief is also very relative. Even without sea anchor, JAMES CAIRD II lies to very well, riding the waves beautifully. We go below and let the boat do the work for us.

The weather does not improve until morning the next day, which marks our sixth day out since leaving Elephant Island. Our position is now 58 degrees 19 minutes south and 052 degrees 33 minutes west. We set all sail and, in light airs, steer 080 degrees. It never ceases to amaze us how quickly the ocean becomes calm. Though still running high, swells, rough and confused only hours earlier, now carry no threat.

On the seventh day the wind shifts to the north-northwest, freshening somewhat. For the first time we can set a direct course for South Georgia. We have already sailed quite far north. As the crow flies, South Georgia is still 489 nautical miles away. We have all sail up and, for a while, move at a five-knot clip. As soon as the weather permits, we throw open the scuttle and let a bit of fresh air below. We can almost cut the air down there with a knife. And yet, compared to Shackleton and the crew of the original JAMES CAIRD, we seem to be living in a regular paradise.

10

On the Knife's Edge

The biggest difference between the 1916 boat journey and ours lies in the number of crewmembers. Shackleton's JAMES CAIRD had a total of six—there are just four of us. Four people on a boat 22-foot long, loaded to the gunwales with provisions, fresh water, equipment and sleeping bags—that's going a little beyond the comfort zone. How Shackleton and his people managed to house six people in the confines of this double-ended lifeboat will always remain a puzzle for me.

The only possible explanation seems to be that three men stayed on deck at all times while the other three lay below trying to find a little rest in their sodden sleeping bags. The man at the helm was relieved every 80 minutes but, after being relieved, he went on sitting in the cockpit. Their foulweather gear had not only been shredded by long use but was also totally unsuited for a journey of this kind. It had been designed for the dry cold of the Antarctic winter, not for a trip in a lifeboat, where it would be drenched by salt water constantly.

The condition of their clothing and—even worse, their sleeping bags—was equally disastrous. Two of the sleeping bags, made of reindeer skin like all the others, began to rot during the voyage. Their sickeningly sweet stench compelled the men to heave the two bags over the side. They took turns using the remaining four bags but even these began shedding their hair in fistfuls. The reindeer hair would then turn up in the men's food, their noses and mouths as well as in every nook and cranny of the boat.

As navigator, Worsley was facing the greatest challenge of his life. In order to work out a fix, he had to find the line of position, which could be determined by accurately measuring the altitude of a star, and by using dead reckoning. Making a sextant sight of the sun from a small boat in the middle of a heaving ocean is no mean feat. To make matters worse, the sun made its appearance only at rare intervals in the whole journey, the sky usually being a mass of clouds.

To compute a fix from the line of position, Worsley had to bring out his waterlogged nautical almanac and logarithm tables to find the desired value. Then, by making handwritten computations, he would arrive at his position. His two books got so wet that the transparent pages stuck together and, after being used just once, would usually disintegrate. Without reliable position fixes, they would not have been able to correct their course. As a result, they might have sailed right past South Georgia into the boundless expanse of the Southern Ocean. When asked where they would go if they missed their landfall, Worsley answered: "To Ireland." The reply was a bit whimsical, as they well knew, but it did express the seriousness of their plight. Missing South Georgia amounted to a death sentence.

Despite this age of the GPS, Martin insists on working with the sextant whenever possible. The rest of us do use the sextant from time to time but not as regularly and conscientiously as Martin. He has had a lot more practice with the sextant than we have. And practice makes perfect. Thumbing his nose at our tiny GPS handsets, Martin plots our course and attempts to work out our position without pocket calculator using only nautical almanac and sextant.

Owing to the cloud cover, opportunities for snapping a sight are few and, mostly, of short duration, so there tends to be rather a long interval between individual sights. That inevitably leads to inaccuracies. Nevertheless, Martin succeeds in working out our position to within 30 nautical miles. Given the accuracy of the GPS nowadays, that may seem ridiculous. But the will and concentration needed to attain those results on a wildly pitching boat can only be appreciated by those who have tried it. Under such conditions even Worsley's navigation would not be much more accurate. That's because snapping a sight with the sextant requires both hands. Martin cannot come to terms with the essential reality of a boat like ours. Time and again, we hear a volley of curses from our usually placid companion.

Assuming Martin has managed to find a halfway secure spot, the problem lies in determining the exact angle between the visual horizon and the star—despite the boat's frenetic motion and the Southern Ocean swells. At the same time, the stopwatch must be stopped at the precise second of the snap, while keeping the sextant from getting wet. Once again, only by teamwork can the job be done. If Martin finally manages to get a satisfactory sight, he can calculate a line of position, but this still doesn't give him the fix. For that, he needs one more snap which should be staggered by a few hours. To review the process: Find a secure place, protect the sextant, hit the stopwatch—unfortunately, all too frequently there is no more sun to be seen, so there is no second reading and as a result no position.

A problem that is causing us more and more concern is that our legs are always cold. We are apparently suffering from poor circulation. This development did not come as any surprise; our predecessors knew all about it. McNeish was the first to have this problem. Sitting in the cockpit on a fairly calm day, he abruptly pulled off one boot and displayed a puffy, dead-white leg and foot. Horrified, the others followed suit and found they all had the same symptoms.

Our seaboots, designed specially for the journey, have kept us warm and dry under the most extreme conditions. But the warmest boots are of no use if the blood ceases to circulate properly. Not only do tight boots adversely affect a person's mental state but they cause debilitating physical problems as well. We're sure of our facts at any rate.

Shackleton, on the other hand, was not always so sure about his decision to sail for South Georgia. His closest companion on JAMES CAIRD was Frank Worsley, the Skipper. At the outset, the Boss kept repeating his reasons for undertaking this perilous mission, in an apparent effort to win approval for the decision. Shackleton's concern for the men marooned on Elephant Island must have made the ordeal of the boat journey all the harder for him. He understood the sea, so he knew exactly what they would be facing.

I often compare his predicament to my 92-day crossing of Antarctica ten years ago during which the idea for this journey came to me. When I announced my plans for the trip in the JAMES CAIRD II, I told a rather surprised public that I considered this expedition far more difficult and dangerous than the crossing of Antarctica. My assessment was borne out in the course of the journey. Familiar with Antarctic conditions, Shackleton came to the same conclusion.

Antarctica is solid land. If explorers have done their homework in preparing and equipping themselves, it is relatively safe terrain. When a gale blows, they just crawl into their tents and wait it out. That's all they have to do. Even in periods of intense cold, life in a tent is not nearly so bad as it may seem; the safety the tent provides is crucial. It's quite another story on the high seas.

The merciless ocean can drive the seafarer to the point of total exhaustion. Being wet and cold at sea is at times much harder to stand than the dry Antarctic cold. Despite extremes on its fringes, the continent itself has stable conditions. In the Southern Ocean, on the other hand, the deck heaves under your feet twenty-four hours a day without respite. At every moment seafarers must live with the fear of being capsized by a rogue wave. They never know what's coming next. On land, adequate planning, conditioning and endurance bring you to the goal. If travelers find themselves exhausted, they can call an occasional time-out. They crawl into their tents to recoup their strength. You cannot do that on the ocean.

In a boat as small as the JAMES CAIRD II, our strength is being sapped from the very start; it will run out, sooner or later. The ocean never lets us relax. This uncertainty gnawing at the psyche and the physical strain imposed by a wildly leaping boat—these two factors push us faster than we suspect to the brink of physical exhaustion.

On Antarctica, we always managed to get our eight hour sleep and, what's more, we slept as blissfully as newborn babies. Out here, we suffer from perpetual sleep deprivation. The knowledge that the ocean is an overwhelming adversary—one that can destroy us at its whim—robs us of any rest. The question is simply whether the ocean will do it or not.

That is why on both voyages—Shackleton's and ours—the element of luck played such an important role. For all their skill, they would never have made South Georgia had Shackleton not been so awfully lucky.

I am fully aware that a lot depends on our luck in this enterprise. Certainly, Force 10 winds are bad. But, undoubtedly, things can get much, much worse. In this part of the world, the ocean never tires of making us look ridiculous, of showing us our own limits. We never win in the struggle with the sea; we can only hope and work—literally—to keep from going under.

Shackleton's decision to make the 700-mile rescue journey to South Georgia in the JAMES CAIRD was controversial for yet another reason: to prepare the lifeboat for such a hazardous voyage, they had to partially dismantle the two other lifeboats, the DUDLEY DOCKER as well as the STANCOMB WILLS. Cannibalized in this way, neither boat could be considered seaworthy any longer. In addition, McNeish, the talented boatbuilder, was going off in the JAMES CAIRD with Shackleton.

Had Sir Ernest's rescue mission failed, those two other lifeboats would have represented the only possibility for the men marooned on Elephant Island to seek help at King George or Deception islands. In fact, Frank Wild's emergency plan called for sailing to Deception Island—in at least one lifeboat. To do so, the castaways would again have to remove the planking of the second boat in order to make a third boat ready for sea. Why—and this question keeps bothering me— didn't they simply try to seek refuge there all together?

The imponderables of a voyage to South Georgia were so great that, even in the desperate situation facing the castaways on Elephant Island, an attempt to make Deception Island in the three lifeboats would have been justified. This awesome responsibility must have been quite clear to Shackleton: Not only did his own life depend on the success of his rescue mission, but so did the lives of every man in the crew.

Our voyage takes place in a different season of the year than the 1916 JAMES CAIRD's journey. The months of April and May can be qualified as winter in the region. On the other hand we are sailing in summer. Even so, we experience cold, we go through blizzards, sleet and hailstorms. The temperature hovers continuously a degree or so above the freezing point and, often, even lower. We are sick and tired of the cold.

We can just imagine how Shackleton, Worsley, McNeish, Crean, McCarthy and Vincent must have frozen in their worn and tattered Burberry overalls, in their slimy, stinking reindeer hide sleeping bags, and in their leaking boots. Water drips in our cabin like a grotto but, on our boat, it's merely condensation. The original JAMES CAIRD leaked from stem to stern, so the exhausted men had to bail around the clock.

We don't need to lie on top of bags of sand and round stones, placed in the bilges of the JAMES CAIRD as ballast; instead, we rest on inflatable, foam-rubber mattresses. Yet, despite this, both crews have very similar impressions.

The peripheral conditions may differ in a few details but we're still talking about the same boat, the same concerns, the same fatigue, the same fears.

On the eighth day we experience stormy weather for the third time since our departure from Elephant Island. At 2300 hours we tuck a reef in the mainsail on a slippery, lurching deck. To do this, we have to get the yard down, so it can't flail around like a huge cudgel. Then, after changing the sheet lead and tucking in the row of reef points, we heave on the halyard in unison, raising the shortened mainsail.

Half an hour later a good Force 8 is blowing, so we have to take in all sail except the mizzen. Once more, we heave to without sea anchor and crawl below. The night is pitch-dark—starless, moonless. There is only this overwhelming blackness out of which towering seas surge beneath us without the slightest warning, seizing our boat and sending her rising to the crest all a-shudder. Then, there's a roar as the comber breaks and comes crashing against the deck over us, only to hurry on, its power undiminished.

Somehow, our tiny boat rides these seas, slipping from under their most punishing blows. God bless that Danish boatbuilder. We know only too well that our lives depend on the boat. But the worst of it is the darkness.

In daylight we can see the rolling mountains of water coming. So, although our heart is in our mouth at the sight of them, at least we're prepared. At night, we are helpless, condemned to sit there idly, waiting for them.

Torsten, who went through the gale aboard the much larger DAGMAR AAEN, is still in awe afterwards: "It's really something when the bow buries itself in the sea and tons of churning water come rolling aft. At the time I stood just abaft the companionway, so I could see forward right to the hawse pipes. We shipped a load of solid green water over the bow. It all happened so fast—it seemed like a second. With a crash, the wave came thundering over the decks, rushing aft to where I was and knocking the pins out from under me. What a wallop that sea packed!"

It is afternoon on the following day before the weather finally improves. We make sail and, in high but orderly swells, resume our course. The wind is out of the west-northwest at Force 7 and pushes us towards South Georgia at a healthy five knots. That seems to be what the JAMES CAIRD II will face.

From time to time, she surfs in huge swells that come up obliquely from astern and run, shuddering, beneath our keel. Though still awesome, the seas now lack the viciousness of the previous nights. Right on course, our double-ender races ahead. If we can keep on making five to seven knots, it will literally catapult us towards our landfall. On the morning of the tenth day we are still 279 miles from our destination, having long since passed the halfway mark. In the evening of the same day we have only 214 miles to go.

Today, at 1830 hours, a meeting of some importance will take place on the high seas. By means of our Inmarsat-C-unit, we have been sending daily position reports to the DAGMAR AAEN. That may sound easy to do—it isn't though.

It's usually in the afternoon, when I'm on stand-by. I climb out of my wet things and try to dry my tender, wrinkled hands. I stretch out on my bunk, using every nook and cranny to wedge myself in. Despite my efforts, I go flying back and forth. With one hand, I pull the watertight case containing the laptop out from behind the bungee cords and, very carefully, to avoid snapping a delicate prong off its plug, I connect the mini-computer to the transmitter and to the power. In doing this, I shield the laptop from any drops of condensation and then, with one finger, try to input our position. It seems as though someone keeps on moving the keyboard back and forth. I keep poking my finger at the thing. It's a wonder that Karsten can even make heads or tails out of the messages I send.

Today the two boats are going to rendezvous—at least, that's the plan—to allow the camera team to film the JAMES CAIRD II on the open ocean.

We are delighted as the familiar silhouette of the DAGMAR AAEN heaves into view, but this meeting disturbs our shipboard routine. We have retreated into the cocoon of our habits. We do this, for one thing, to get our minds off the awful living conditions aboard the JAMES CAIRD II and, for another, to sail the boat as efficiently as possible.

To us the rendezvous becomes an intrusion, a violation of our personal space. It doesn't help us; it's just a nuisance. In comparison to the JAMES CAIRD II, the DAGMAR AAEN looks as solid and indestructible as some 10,000-ton vessel. And she probably is just that. At times, her entire hull disappears in a wave trough, so only the truck of her mast projects over the crest. Then she takes another elevator ride and, for a second, her entire gleaming wet bow emerges from the water; we even glimpse the forward part of her keel. She goes back down in the next wave trough, so only her crow's-nest and red-and-white pennant can be seen.

It's quite a spectacle, one that very clearly demonstrates the height of the swells. The DAGMAR AAEN circles us a few times. Coming any closer in this seaway would be far too dangerous. Propped up by Georg and Tim, Ralf stands on deck, filming the tiny JAMES CAIRD II. On deck are Karsten, Katja, Torsten, Ute, Uschi and Jürgen—they're all there, waving and taking pictures. At the end of about an hour, the gam is over. The DAGMAR AAEN resumes her course and soon disappears.

We are again alone, as if it had never been any other way. That is as it should be. The rendezvous may have brought a certain relief to our families for, shortly thereafter, they receive the glad tidings that apparently we are as well as could be expected. We, however, are so wrapped up in our own world that our thoughts seldom drift homewards.

11

Storm and Ice

It seems as though the worst is behind us. The wind is blowing steadily out of the west-northwest at Force 4-6, in the right direction. We have grown accustomed to the big ocean swell, but not to our dank, cramped quarters below. In the last few days the temperature has risen somewhat, and it makes itself pleasantly felt. At night, we sail under the starlit canopy of the heavens; during the day, we are accompanied by sun and cumulus clouds, the barometric pressure having attained its highest reading of the entire voyage. Things are looking up again, particularly in view of the fact that our boat journey is making rapid progress towards its goal—South Georgia.

On the evening of the eleventh day we are still 113 miles from Cape Rosa, the headland marking the entrance to King Haakon Bay. We are steering for this bay since it was here that Shackleton made first landfall after completing the passage. With the present weather and wind direction, we could make South Georgia's north side—sheltered from wind and waves—but that wouldn't be authentic. Originally, Shackleton had planned to round the island. But the wind, the condition of the boat, as well as the men's exhaustion, made it imperative to get ashore as soon as possible. At this point, none of them, not even Sir Ernest, was contemplating the idea of making an arduous trek across South Georgia to seek help on the other side. King Haakon Bay was therefore the first possibility of reaching land although this would in the end nearly result in disaster.

The situation aboard the JAMES CAIRD was utterly desperate. Their last cask of fresh water had gone brackish. Apparently, in the course of provisioning the lifeboat at Elephant Island, this cask was stove in; the water was now so salty and foul tasting that the men could hardly drink it. They suffered terribly from thirst.

Compounding their problems was the question of whether Worsley's calculations were in fact correct. The possibility that they had already sailed past South Georgia tortured them. Missing a landfall, of course, meant death since the JAMES CAIRD could not turn and beat back to windward. That is something that we, on JAMES CAIRD II, have witnessed with our own eyes a number of times.

Whatever the cost, they had to make landfall on the island—or die. There was no other alternative. But even the first choice could scarcely be called tempting. South Georgia is an extremely mountainous island with sheer cliffs, reefs and treacherous currents. Even today its coast remains partially uncharted. There were neither lighthouses nor buoys in those times and none today for that matter. Rising like a great dark block, the island repels the onslaught of the endless seas which thunder against its cliffs.

All seafarers fear this iron-bound coast and always make sure to put as much sea-room as possible between it and themselves. Nonetheless, Shackleton had to risk a landing there, their plight allowing no further delay. For want of proper oakum and tar, McNeish had caulked the boat's seams with lamp-wick and penguins' blood, so now she was leaking badly. They knew that the boat could sink any day. Time was working against them—staying at sea even one more day could be fatal.

We intend to retrace the route of the historic expedition as closely as possible. For the sake of authenticity, this means making a landing on that exposed stretch of south coast— with all the nasty consequences it may entail. Clearly, weather conditions are subject to change. The wind that blew one way for Shackleton may come from the opposite compass quadrant for us. Visibility, wind velocity, seaway—these are all variable factors. The matter of a "wrong side" landing on South Georgia has been of the greatest concern to us, right from the earliest planning stages. We would be delighted to sail around the northwestern tip of the island and make our landing in complete safety on the sheltered side.

In 1993, Trevor Potts, an Englishman, re-enacted the stretch from Elephant Island to South Georgia aboard his modern epoxy replica of the JAMES CAIRD. We must bear in mind, though, that he had left out the first leg of the journey. Also, for safety's sake, he rounded South Georgia's west cape so he could make a sheltered landing. He didn't trek across the island, either. Since we intend to retrace the historic crossing, we must begin at Shackleton's point of departure.

Just like Shackleton and his five companions, we search the horizon constantly for the first signs of land. We notice decidedly more birds—among them, the enormous wandering albatross, which nest on South Georgia. With a wingspan of over nine feet, these birds glide without even flapping their wings, as if they had annulled the law of gravity.

Worsley's calculations put the island a mere 12 nautical miles away. The castaways should have made out its high mountain peaks long before this, but the visibility was so poor that they could see only a few miles. Doubts about sailing past the island and fears of running into the island's granite walls must have been almost unbearable. Finally, it was McCarthy who first sighted land, no more than ten miles dead ahead. His hoarse cry of "Land Ho!" gladdened the hearts of his exhausted comrades. Worsley had done it. Given the circumstances, finding this remote island represents an incredible feat of navigation, one that has few parallels in the annals of seafaring.

At last, their goal was within reach, but they would not rest on their oars for long. Quite the contrary, despite the unspeakable relief this moment must have brought them. These six had achieved the impossible, they had managed something daring beyond belief. But just three miles off the coast they met the violence of that rock-bound coast.

Instead of being able to round South Georgia's northwestern tip, which would have meant safety, they encountered huge cross swells building up abruptly. These confused seas tossed the lifeboat around like a toy, setting her farther and farther to the southeast. They could already see the greenish tussock grass, they could smell the land—but were unable to attempt a landing with the running surf. In a split-second their boat would have been smashed to kindling wood, and not one of them would have survived. They must have recognized the menace even in their state of exhaustion. They longed desperately to feel solid land under their feet again, but the ocean was not yet done with them. A terrifying finale lay in store for them.

Not far away they could see blind rollers that were breaking over reefs not shown on any chart. Worse still, the weather began deteriorating and, before they knew it, they were in one of the worst gales they had seen so far. The short winter day gave way to a pitch-black night full of dread. To attempt a landing in that seaway would have been suicidal. Unwilling to believe they could be so near and yet unable to reach land, they bore off and headed back out to sea. When they had sufficient sea room, they hove to, waiting for the next day.

Meanwhile the wind was blowing up. What the exact velocity was no one can say with certainty, as the men of those days had no reliable anemometers. They did have the Beaufort scale for determining wind speed by the sea condition, and experienced seafarers could draw conclusions about wind velocity based on the appearance of the sea. This, of course, is only a crude system, one that relies heavily on subjectivity.

Near South Georgia's coast, where there are cross swells and katabatic winds, it is particularly difficult to get a reliable measurement. The stronger the wind, the more difficult it becomes to obtain an accurate report. However, it is safe to say that the wind reached Force 10, corresponding to at least 50 knots and that, subsequently, it increased from gale to hurricane strength. If riding out the gale hove-to were not enough, the wind was inexorably sending Shackleton's boat onto a lee shore.

Had they failed to gain enough sea room, the lifeboat would have been dashed against the sheer granite cliffs, with results comparable to going over Niagara Falls. Under closely-reefed sails, they somehow managed to claw off shore. But beating to windward in a hurricane with a boat like the JAMES CAIRD is next to impossible. Making that much leeway, they barely managed to weather the rocks of Annenkov Island. Grimly taking bearings, with the lifeboat close-hauled, Worsley and Shackleton realized the futility of their struggle. Worsley wrote: "As we looked at that hellish rock-bound coast, with its roaring breakers, we wondered, impersonally, at which spot our end was to come." And, with a note of regret, he added: "No one would ever know we had got so far."

Without seeking to detract from their achievement— something that stands above all doubt—they lived through this worst of all storms only thanks to a caprice of nature. Their bearings on the foaming cliffs of Annenkov Island suddenly began to change. They would actually clear the dark craggy mass. Some merciful current had seized the JAMES CAIRD, giving her the one last push needed to escape destruction.

It is a miracle that they survived the storm. The pounding into head seas caused the caulking to disintegrate and allowed water to come in through every seam. The tired men had to keep bailing constantly. Then, just as the storm finally abated, the pin securing the heel of the mainmast came loose. If this had happened an hour earlier, the mast would have snapped like a matchstick and nothing in the world could have saved them from drowning.

On May 10, 1916, they finally reached King Haakon Bay and, in a sheltered cove there, they ran the bow of the JAMES CAIRD ashore on the gravel beach. One year, five months and seven days after sailing for the Antarctic in the ENDURANCE, they again stood on South Georgia. They had made their landfall 17 days after leaving Elephant Island.

If I am worried about making for this coast, it is not only because of our predecessors' experience. South Georgia produces weather all its own, weather totally unpredictable that often strikes without warning. We would gladly steer a rather northerly course to give those sinister cliffs a wide berth, but then we needn't have set out on this voyage in the first place. Once more, we encourage each other and stick by our decision. In doing so, it is almost as if the events are repeating themselves. With one exception: We run into ice. Not just some kind of bergy bits or growlers, but gigantic icebergs and fields of drift ice, all of which stem from a single cause: an immense tabular berg.

According to our estimates this colossus, which must be 300 to 400 square miles, formed by calving from the Antarctic shelf ice some time ago and has been drifting like a floating island since then. Only the Shag Rocks, cliffs lying northwest of South Georgia, have checked its progress. After stranding itself there, the table berg has begun to disintegrate. In recent years there have been repeated warnings about such tabular bergs and several reports of sightings, even on our expedition. It is hard to say whether they simply drifted through the ocean unnoticed by ship traffic in earlier times or whether global warming has propagated them. As countless ships plied these waters in the days of whaling, it is rather unlikely that the bergs had gone unsighted. There were and still are small icebergs and bergy bits along South Georgia's coasts. The density of the icebergs that we are encountering is quite unusual. As far as the eye can see, icebergs of all sizes drift. They bear down on us with growlers and sparkling ice fields in tow, compelling us to evasive maneuvers, even this far from the coast.

When setting out from Elephant Island, Shackleton's concern with ice prompted him to sail as far north as possible before heading east. "Of all the threats, ice represents the greatest one," he said. That is especially true at night. After making it through the belt of ice around Elephant Island, they encountered no further ice on the entire journey.

All at once, we no longer know which way to turn, as JAMES CAIRD II cannot sail through all the loose ice. DAGMAR AAEN would go through this concentration without a second thought, but then the DAGMAR AAEN is ice-reinforced and of incredibly solid construction.

As long as the visibility holds and the wind stays moderate, we can hold our own in this slalom course. But the visibility diminishes as the day goes on. The fog rolls in and we can no longer make out the bergs until they are only a few hundred yards away. Nevertheless, we still have enough time to react although steering a direct course among the bergs is not always possible. Another problem arises: At times we must sail between two icebergs and find ourselves becalmed in the lee of one of them. Without wind in our sails, we roll dreadfully in the rough sea. What's worse, we go drifting smack into the leeward berg. Their flanks are hollowed out, eroded like grottoes. Flinging spray, huge ocean swells crash into these caves, cracking off great chunks of ice with each blow. The grottoes are so big that the JAMES CAIRD II could sail right in, mast and all. Of course, it would be wrecked in a matter of minutes. The first wave would pick the boat up, so that her mast trucks would ram into the ice ceiling. Like spears, the butt ends of the masts would go through the bottom of the boat. She would break up and sink. Just a single wave would suffice to turn our boat into flotsam and jetsam— and the four of us into corpses. The danger looms up so suddenly and is so terrible that we all strive to keep clear of these wind shadows. That windward iceberg, the one that steals our wind, keeps getting closer. It's as though we have a choice—either to be smashed to smithereens in an ice grotto or be overrun and pushed under water. The loose, crumbling ice surrounding our hull holds it back like a parking brake. Rowing gains us no ground. We take bearings, trim the sails, curse and try to take advantage of the least breath of wind. It's like being in a railway shunting yard between two locomotives that are rolling towards each other. The grottoes are getting closer together and so are the windward bergs. We are growing desperate. Then Martin looks up, quizzically. A breath of wind has stroked his beard. Yes, he seems convinced. Very slowly, the boat pushes its way through the ice field—just in time. As we near a hollow in the windward iceberg, the wind grabs us with its full force. The JAMES CAIRD II heels, picks up speed and, minutes later, sails clear of the danger zone.

Dazed by the experience, we sight more icebergs ahead. We are still 80 nautical miles from Cape Rosa and the sea is already choked with ice.

On the twelfth day since leaving Elephant Island we sight land on the horizon at 10:00 a.m. At least we think it's land. The distance to Cape Rosa is some 60 miles, so that would do it. In good visibility, the high peaks can be seen that far away. An hour later we have to revise our opinion. It isn't land we've seen—it's ice! Like a tremendous barrier the ice field stretches along the horizon, and all at once we realize that the hardest test still lies ahead.

Apart from the fact that we are better equipped than Shackleton was, the disappointment is as great for us as it must have been for him and his men. They too yearned to be ashore and in safety when the storm hit. And what about us? The weather has been favorable for the past two days. The wind gave us our two best daily runs for the whole trip and we really thought it was going to stay that way. Why shouldn't it? Hadn't we been tested enough?

The wind keeps on blowing from the north at Force 7. It has strengthened somewhat, the sea is running high again, but we are moving along nicely. If only there were no fog. Impenetrably thick areas of fog gather all of a sudden, turning the ocean and the icebergs floating in it to a leaden gray. Our maximum visibility is now 50 yards— far too little to maneuver the sluggish JAMES CAIRD II safely through the icebergs. Our kingdom for a radar set, and that goes double for a motor. JAMES CAIRD II has neither of them. It is as though the sea wanted to put us through one last test, compliments of Shackleton and Worsley. The barometer does not augur well. The air pressure is dropping fast and when it starts drizzling to boot, the pea soup is perfect.

I hear from the DAGMAR AAEN over our Inmarsat unit that she is waiting for us in King Haakon Bay. Karsten warns us urgently about the iceberg menace. Even the DAGMAR AAEN, equipped with a powerful diesel engine and a radar set, had trouble picking her way into the fjord. Now, in winds that are strengthening more and more, she is tacking into the inlet, trying desperately to find a halfway secure anchorage.

At 1600 hours we have to reef the main. With the thick cloud cover and the fog, it is growing dark even earlier than usual. Visibility is so poor that we only see the icebergs when they are dead ahead. All of us are on deck now trying to see through the fog, but it is hard to see anything. Again and again, we have to make turns that are just plain foolhardy. We gybe every few minutes to get clear of the bergs. No sooner have we outmaneuvered one than a new one looms. In the next few hours we head this way and that off the coast—out of sheer desperation. Even though we are in the entrance to King Haakon Bay, we are unable to see the slightest sign of land. Dead ahead, where we were to sail according to the compass, lies an impenetrable ice barrier. We are at our destination but cannot make landfall. Instead, the wind strengthens drastically in the next half hour. We make it to be Force 8, coupled with growing darkness, fog, omnipresent bergs. Without the ice, we would certainly be in the fjord within the next hour, but proceeding under these conditions is inviting disaster. We discuss the situation and decide to run back. We have plotted our course coming into the bay, and we can use it in reverse. Some 10 to 15 miles seaward we sailed through an area relatively ice-free compared to the rest of the ice concentration. We mean to go back there and wait for the weather to improve.

For the moment, however, the weather is deteriorating steadily. As we try to find clear water among the bergs, we are inwardly preparing for the worst. The night, which is descending upon us, is oppressively black. We cannot see the ice until it is a few yards away. Finally, we take in the mainsail and heave to under storm jib and mizzen. Our concerns over ice, the cliffs of South Georgia and the gathering storm prevent us from finding any rest.

12

Ice Cold

I don't know how we get through the night without hitting an iceberg. At day break, we lie on a heaving ocean among these awesome, gleaming giants. We have been so close to some bergs that collision seemed certain. It is more luck than seamanship that we survived the night unscathed.

The morning is not promising, and we get the feeling that fate is playing a game of cat and mouse with us. We had hoped that the storm would at least drive away the fog, but it persists just as stubbornly as the day before. It's enough to make us cry. At 1000 hours, we estimate the wind at Force 9, or 42 knots. By noon, we have a full gale, with Force 10 winds, equivalent to at least 50 knots. Our situation is now worse than serious. We consider the idea of taking a really wild run to the southeast. With the northwest gale that's blowing, we could swing around South Georgia's southern tip and be in safety there. There's a lot to be said for the idea— namely, the fact that fewer bergs lie to the south. At any rate, we get that impression in the brief moments when the fog lifts.

But that would mean eliminating the trek across South Georgia, a trek we are determined to do. The situation is totally absurd. We are crouching in a tiny boat among icebergs in the midst of a storm, debating our crossing of the island. But it's unanimous—we all want that crossing, just as we had all wanted the voyage. Rationally speaking, we may not be able to do it, any more than the entire journey can be relived for that matter, and yet, once again, our stubbornness wins out. We intend to reach our self-imposed goal. So we resume course and, as best we can, head back for the coast and King Haakon Bay.

Wedged between deck and bunk, using my sleeping bag to absorb the pounding, I lie on my side trying to send an e-mail to Karsten. To accomplish this, I must keep my knees between mast and ceiling. Then, holding the laptop with my left hand, I use my right forefinger to grope for the correct key. The way the boat is bouncing around, this becomes a test of dexterity and patience. I am satisfied with a success ratio of one hit for three tries. Somehow I manage to input the short message and send it. Thirty minutes later I have Karsten's answer.

Our plan—discussed so briefly—calls for the DAGMAR AAEN to meet us for reasons of safety. If necessary, she will lead us through the ice fields. In spite of the foul weather, the cutter weighs anchor at once and heads out to sea. According to Karsten, the wind is blowing Force 10 *inside* King Haakon Bay. The crew of the DAGMAR AAEN gets ready for a rough trip.

Meanwhile, we do our best to make up for the ground lost the night before. Maybe we should have arranged to rendezvous with the DAGMAR AAEN at the entrance to the bay yesterday, but we were still hoping the weather might improve. Since then, it has only grown worse. If we had met outside the bay half a day sooner, we could have run for its shelter with the following wind and good visibility. If only this, if only that. All that kind of second guessing is futile.

We haven't slept; we are tired, wet and cold. The boat's motion is sickening. Curiously, though, none of us is actually seasick. For days now, our only nourishment has been Power Bars and Peronin. We have had far too little food or drink. For fear of another trip to the head, we refrain from eating and drinking. We need to put more food and liquids in our bodies. But we don't. We all feel rotten. Our hands look like those on a drowning victim—dead-white, swollen. The skin is wrinkled and chapped with the consistency of a bath sponge.

Sigga and Henryk suffer the most, for their bunks have been drenched. While Martin and I have damp sleeping bags, the sleeping quarters of the other two are quite exposed. At regular intervals, they receive a deluge of seawater coming down the hatchway. Both their faces are gaunt, with dark circles under their eyes. Martin and I don't look any better.

Why are we doing this to ourselves? We're at the end of our rope. Why aren't we sitting on the HANSEATIC or the BREMEN looking at the scenery over the rim of a cocktail glass? In this kind of situation, wondering about the meaning of our actions saps our vitality. We need every last ounce of energy to get through this situation.

What we're doing is frankly useless—it serves no practical purpose. But it makes us feel good. We couldn't wait to get out here—even though that's something we hardly believe now, in our present misery. It is only because we have chosen

to come that we can endure the situation. Anyone forced
into this part of the voyage would soon have died of fright,
despair, cold or exhaustion.

"It is incredible what human determination can accomplish. The spirit pervades the body, creating an active state
that repels all harmful influences," said Goethe. Although I
somehow doubt that Goethe ever got himself in a jam like
this, he was right. The human will does move mountains. If
we have withstood these last days and nights, it is mainly
thanks to our will power. We all worked so long and hard for
the journey that we have become totally identified with it. We
are now drawing energy from it. There is potential energy
that cannot be called on demand but affects the will deci-
sively. We want something and the more it hurts, the greater
our will. It's like the saying: "You got yourself into this mess,
now see what you can do to get yourself out in one piece."

People have asked me if I'm religious or turn to religion
in such moments of peril. The assumption is that, in times of
crisis, we seek refuge by praying to a higher being. I would
neither describe myself as an atheist nor a believer in an ec-
umenical sense. For me, God is creation, what I see around
me. I believe in the laws of nature. I see in nature itself a
higher authority from which all of us stem, including our
time on earth; an authority to which we have subordinated
ourselves and one to which at some time we will also return.
But I don't believe in living my life in accordance with that. I
can't really get into church doctrine. Apart from the fact that
a 22-foot boat in a storm is hardly the place for silent prayers,
I wouldn't do it as I don't believe in it and would even
consider it an act of cowardice.

There is no room for such considerations just now. We

say little to each other—not because we have nothing to say but because we are just too tired. There is no time for philosophical contemplation during the voyage. This urge becomes all the stronger afterwards. After all my trips, I draw up a kind of adventure balance sheet. Not only is every moment of agony, such as the one we are facing now, entered in the ledger; I also review the many highpoints, the positive impressions and, finally, the feeling of having done it. *Ad astra per aspera*, through hardship to the stars. There's something to that wise saying. For me, the positive elements have always been dominant. I don't undertake these expeditions because of some masochistic streak.

We are waging an all or nothing struggle in the same spot as our predecessors. My dread of this coast, something that I'd felt long before embarking on this journey, seems almost a vision. It's just the way I'd pictured it in my worst dreams and, yet, it is all as it was meant to be. Shackleton and his group had far more wind at this precise spot than we do; in exchange, we have lots of ice. Then as now, the visibility was bad.

Certainly, our boat is holding her own, but that could all change in one second if we were to collide with a piece of ice. It's ice—not the storm—that we fear the most. The four of us have years of experience in the ice. We know what ice can do. Perhaps those with less experience would view this threat with more composure. Even when we are relatively sheltered from the outside, crouching below decks trying to warm our frozen suffering hands, we never forget that 3/4-inch-thick planking is all that separates us from the ice. The thumps and scraping noises when even small chunks strike the hull terrify us.

We meet the DAGMAR AAEN near the entrance to the bay. It is evening again. Our mother ship carries storm jib and try-sail, canvas that we set only in the heaviest kind of weather. Although I have owned DAGMAR AAEN for twelve years, I have never seen her from afar during a storm. I have always been on board. Her sea-going qualities are well-known. She pitches and rolls but takes little green water aboard while riding the seas with incredible grace. You get the feeling that she's actually enjoying herself, that she's in her element in the roughest weather. Her strength and the trust it engenders are heart warming.

There's something reassuringly professional about the way the crew work as they handle sheets and canvas on the pitching deck. Karsten, at the helm, circles the JAMES CAIRD II a few times. It is shortly before nightfall and the intensity of the storm has clearly diminished. There is no possibility of entering the bay in a storm at night. Because of the heavy seas the ice can hardly be identified, even on the DAGMAR AAEN's radar screen.

The radar monitor is showing white everywhere, even with the seaway suppression filter turned on. Karsten puts two lookouts on the bow using search lights, but it is still too dangerous to enter the bay. We decide to heave to overnight. To do this, we plan to use a connecting line, not the easiest thing to do in Force 10 winds. All attempts from the DAGMAR AAEN to send over a heaving line fail and, at times, the big cutter comes threateningly close to JAMES CAIRD II. Finally, we decide on another tactic. From JAMES CAIRD II we float a long line with the buoy from our sea anchor down to the DAG-MAR AAEN and they pick it up with a boathook. We then haul in their warp and make it fast to our forward cleat. When that is done, the DAGMAR AAEN heads up into the wind holding us in position 150 yards off her stern.

This supposedly easy, straightforward maneuver takes several backbreaking hours with the four of us in survival suits, crawling over the deck, our eyes burning from salt water, our hands numb from handling wet lines and rigging.

The crew of the DAGMAR AAEN are not doing much better. They are sodden and cold. The lookouts on the bow have a particularly tough time. Every time the cutter's bow buries itself in a sea, cascades of icy water wash over them. I have no idea how many tons of water there are in a breaking sea or how much kinetic force it packs. Although the lookouts are securely harnessed, they are continually being knocked off their feet.

Unflappable, Katja, Uschi and Ute go about their work as if heaving-to in a gale off South Georgia were the most natural thing in the world. Despite the heavy weather, Ralf, Georg and Tim keep on filming with their state-of-the-art digital camera as if they were attending the boat races at home. Torsten takes pictures, while Jürgen acts as lookout and accepts getting drenched with stoicism, and an imperturbable Karsten is at the helm. The success or failure of a project always depends on the professionalism and spirit of the crew. One thing is sure—we couldn't have wished for a better support team.

As darkness falls over us, the worst night in my seafaring life begins. With renewed fury, the storm howls; in the meantime, heavy seas have built up. We see only the stern light of the DAGMAR AAEN, and the eerie searchlight with which her crew uninterruptedly combs the sea for ice. This ghostly light, which suddenly dies in the troughs of the waves to reappear as a pale shadow on the next wave before moving upward to the crest of a 15- or 16-foot sea, burns itself indelibly in my memory. Over and over, the DAGMAR AAEN is forced to take evasive action as the beam of the searchlight bounces straight back from a gleaming block of ice.

Breaking seas wash completely over JAMES CAIRD II. Their impact causes physical pain, taking our breath away. We are covered with spray and cannot see anything without glasses. We try wearing dark ski goggles but that makes everything look blacker and, within seconds, the lenses are covered with salt. We have pulled the drawstrings of our facemasks and hoods so tight that only narrow eye slits are left for us to squint through to make sure we are maintaining our position astern of the DAGMAR AAEN. Although a line connects us, we are constantly threatened with a broach-going broadside to the waves—which could end in a capsize. On the open ocean, we would now bring out our sea anchor, secure the hatch, and wait the storm out below. Doing that here—off the coast, amid ice fields—we might just as well chop a hole in the hull ourselves.

I cannot recall ever experiencing such a dark, interminable night. Sigga, on deck from 1800 to 2100 hours, goes through the worst time in her entire sailing career. And that's saying something, for Sigga is not easily fazed. The seas crash into us with such force that, below decks, it sounds like the whole boat is coming apart. Henryk, whom I relieve at midnight, looks totally desperate. He has never been so cold in his life as on this watch. Never a complainer even when the going gets rough, he now starts crying, cursing the weather. He is totally exhausted. So am I. This angry ocean, the knowledge that danger and physical suffering are at hand, exhaust our last reserves of strength.

Never have three hours dragged by so slowly. Every couple of minutes, I tell myself that my watch must be over, but every damned second stretches out interminably. A succession of fragmentary pictures dance in my mind's eye, pictures of earlier voyages, of critical situations. When Martin finally relieves me, I can only think of getting below.

For him, too, this night is at the limits of the endurable. No sailor job is too hard for Martin. Unlike any of us, he is constantly adjusting the trim of the sails, trying to heat water; or else, he's at the tiller singing in his rich, melodious voice. Suddenly he has become monosyllabic; he too complains about being cold and wet.

What a picture of misery we must be, barely keeping JAMES CAIRD II above water. But even this night has to end. During Martin's watch the day breaks and when Sigga takes over from him, the wind drops appreciably. Toward noon, wind and seaway fall off so much that, together with the DAGMAR AAEN, we can resume our run into King Haakon Bay. For the first time, we see land today. The storm is over. A bit later, South Georgia lies bathed in sunlight before us: green mountain slopes, glaciers and snow-draped peaks, with seals and penguins in the water. A truly peaceful image. As in the interim the wind has dropped off to a flat calm, we allow the DAGMAR AAEN to tow us to the head of King Haakon Bay.

We want to go to Peggotty Camp, the site from which Shackleton, Worsley and Crean left on the last and decisive phase of their rescue mission—the trek across the mountainous island.

*   *   *

As the DAGMAR AAEN drops anchor at the farthest end of the bay and we ghost alongside her, we can hardly get used to the quiet. We are totally exhausted and yet bursting with excitement. Our gait is stiff, jerky, uncoordinated; we move as if drunk. At last, we can stand again, stretch our legs, get rid of our wet, stinking clothes and sit at a proper table, eat and drink. We are in a daze. Our delight at having re-enacted the boat journey is overwhelming. But we express it guardedly, as if we fear our joy may burst over us uncontrollably.

We are dead tired. We all feel an aversion for the JAMES CAIRD II. Nobody wants to go back aboard. Nothing in the world will get Henryk, Sigga or Martin to spend another night on our cockleshell. The boat brought us here safe and sound but, in return, demanded everything from us. Yet we know all too well that things could have been much worse. Just like Shackleton, Worsley, Crean, McCarthy, Vincent and McNeish, we were lucky.

13

A Mountain Marathon

Measuring roughly 110 miles long and 20 miles at its widest part, the island has the form of an oversized breakwater. In contrast to the sheltered northern coast, the south coast—exposed to wind and wave—appears desolate, bleak, weather-beaten. From the snow-clad interior, glacial tongues spread down steep, bare slopes into the valleys, with odd clumps of tussock grass sprouting only in marshy flats. In Shackleton's time, the island's craggy peaks were regarded as impassable and had not yet been crossed. After all, why cross such mountains when all the whaling stations were on the island's sheltered north side?

For Shackleton and his five men, reaching any whaling station by sea meant going a further 130 nautical miles. None of the castaways would give this idea a second thought. They had survived the boat journey by the skin of their teeth and no power on earth could induce them to go back on the open ocean, even if only for a coastwise passage. The trials of the previous weeks had marked them deeply, and the JAMES CAIRD had suffered too much damage.

In landing at Camp Cove, they'd had to lighten the ship, as the exhausted men found it impossible to pull their heavily laden lifeboat out of the surf. They had found a cove which sheltered them from wind and weather, but the JAMES CAIRD took a severe beating in the surf. She lost her rudder and, pounding against the rocks, was nearly stove-in. McNeish had to cut away her decking and the upper planking so the men could drag her up to safety. Even after she was lightened, hours of backbreaking work were needed to haul the lifeboat higher up the beach.

The JAMES CAIRD was an open boat again, and a seriously weakened one at that. She could not be expected to make another sea voyage, not even along the coast.

The new campsite seemed like paradise on earth. Solid land underfoot again! A cave that gave shelter and kept them dry. And there was food in abundance. Even more important than food was fresh water. They could finally slake their terrible thirst at a little stream that babbled right next to their camp. Roosting on the slopes above them were hundreds of albatrosses, and the fledglings in their nests represented a source of delicious food. The half-starved men gorged themselves on the young birds they stewed, savoring the rich broth until sated, exhausted, they fell into a deep sleep. Afterwards, they ate again and then slept once more.

When, after a few days, they had regained their strength, Shackleton began to make his plans. Camp Cove was too isolated. In order to go for help on the other side of South Georgia, he had to traverse the island's rough upland—by hook or by crook. To do this, he would need to find a better jumping-

On April 24, 1915, Shackleton and a small crew depart from Point Wild on the lifeboat JAMES CAIRD in a desperate attempt to reach South Georgia. *Royal Geographic Society, London*

After a three-hour watch, I go below, wet and cold, where I face another three hours of stand-by watch. *Henryk Wolski*

The desperate situation of Shackleton's crew is made dramatically clear by these pictures. The 22 men spent four months on the rocky outcrop, suffering from the cold and stormy conditions and waiting for Shackleton's return. *Brigitte Ellerbrock* (top) *Torsten Heller* (bottom)

JAMES CAIRD II in heavy weather. The boat is so small that the stormy seas make it appear as if we sit in the water. *Torsten Heller*

Finally a beautiful day and the wind helps to make good progress. These moments make up for the hardships. *Torsten Heller*

The elephant seals don't' seem to be impressed by our feat. *Torsten Heller*

This is the natural habitat of the penguins. They feel right at home even on the steepest and most forbidding ice walls. *Torsten Heller*

In heavy weather Ralf Gemmecke works his way forward on the DAGMAR AAEN. *Torsten Heller*

Under reefed main, DAGMAR AAEN battles heavy seas. *Torsten Heller*

Sailing among the icebergs requires tremendous concentration. As beautiful as they look, they are extremely dangerous for the sailor. *Torsten Heller*

King Haakon Bay. After the stormy passage, even glaciered-covered South Georgia looks like the Promised Land. We cannot wait to start our crossing. *Torsten Heller*

We begin our trek at the very same spot where Shackleton established Pegotty Camp. Our backpacks weight about 50 pounds, a heavy load after the long boat journey. *Torsten Heller*

Crossing South Georgia on foot, we are passing Shackleton Gap. *Torsten Heller*

Negotiating the glaciers requires careful maneuvering. *Torsten Heller*

Finally we are approaching the old whaling station of Stromness.
It was on this path in 1916 that Shackleton, Crean and Worsley reached
the station after their 36-hour ordeal. *Torsten Heller*

off point. In other words, they would strike camp and seek a new one, further into King Haakon Bay.

On May 15, they launched the JAMES CAIRD loading her with all their gear and, with a favoring breeze, sailed toward the head of the bay. The trip they had was wonderfully relaxed. The men even began singing, generous portions of albatross stew and a good rest having restored them. At midday, they reached the head of the bay and ran the boat ashore on a wide beach. Around them basked hundreds of sea elephants and fur seals, promising food in abundance.

Again they unloaded the JAMES CAIRD. Then she was hauled up onto the beach and turned over. There, McCarthy used stones to build a kind of foundation, atop of which the upturned boat formed a roof. They called the place "Peggotty Camp," after the character by that name in Dickens' *David Copperfield.*

Frank Worsley would later write about an interesting phenomenon: in a wide radius around their camp, the men encountered great quantities of driftwood that must have come from wrecked ships—masts, yards, bulwarks, splintered planking, figureheads—all lying jumbled together on the beach. Apparently, a current carried this wreckage from far-off Cape Horn all the way to the head of King Haakon Bay where it washed up on this stretch of beach.

After settling into their new quarters, the men began preparations for crossing the island on foot. Aside from Shackleton himself, the imperturbable Worsley—once again, in charge of navigation—and Tom Crean would be making the trek. With his powerful physique, Crean was not only the strongest man in the group, but had also gained experience in ice and snow as a member of Scott's overland expedition to the South Pole. In fact, he was the last to have seen Scott alive.

McNeish, left in charge of the men staying behind at Peggotty Camp, drove eight screws into each of the three climbers' bootsoles, creating makeshift crampons. Putting McNeish in charge can only be considered a clever move on Shackleton's part, for he held the boatbuilder in low esteem. The dour middle-aged carpenter had a reputation for stirring up hard feelings with his natural pessimism and abrasive manner. Thus, by making McNeish responsible, Shackleton sought to head off any discord during his absence, binding the man by his honor and sense of commitment.

In terms of equipment, the climbers would carry only the bare essentials. They left behind tent and sleeping bags, taking only one Primus stove, enough fuel for three days, and one saucepan. In addition, each man was to carry his own provisions. Finally, their equipment would include about 90 feet of well-worn rope, a carpenter's adze (to serve as an ice axe), two compasses, a telescope as well as a supply of matches. The only map of this region had been made by Filchner's expedition a few years earlier. The castaways had a copy of this German map.

As accurate as it was, the map covered only South Georgia's coastal regions. How the interior looked or whether there was in fact any way over the mountains, or where it might be, remained matters of pure speculation.

That these six had survived the boat journey comes close to being a tale from *The Arabian Nights*. But then to have crossed South Georgia with equipment that, even for those times, could only be termed pathetic, is a second miracle, one rivaling the first.

The weather on this whalers' island is remarkable for its unpredictable storms, which set in with a suddenness and viciousness that can blow travelers caught unawares right off the glaciers. As the three climbers left behind tent and sleeping bags, they deprived themselves of any possibility of finding shelter or surviving storms of any duration. They also failed to carry along a shovel with which they might have tunneled into a snowdrift. Were they to fall foul of bad weather—the likelihood of which is very great on South Georgia—they would certainly have perished. The men must have been perfectly aware of this. By dispensing with any possibility of an overnight stay Shackleton was putting himself and his companions under an enormous constraint. There would be no halts, except for cooking and those short breathers that were absolutely necessary. This was a kind of Russian roulette. Any sudden drop in temperature, an impassable spot in uncharted, hitherto unexplored country would have spelled delay and, hence, their doom. Given these conditions, the risks they had decided to take were staggering.

Were there alternatives to their course of action? Shackleton's haste was not prompted by his concerns for the crew of the JAMES CAIRD so much as by his fears for the men marooned on Elephant Island. After their rest ashore, he and his five companions had bounced back fairly well. At any rate, they were under no time constraint. They had fresh water, food and fuel available in unlimited quantity. In contrast, life on Elephant Island must have been frightful in the Antarctic winter. Now there were few seals or penguins around, as these creatures head for open ocean during the winter. The castaways' desperate plight, their uncertainty as to whether the JAMES CAIRD had reached her goal or whether there were any ships in this season for a rescue mission, must have tortured them.

They had a great deal of time in which to mull over their predicament. Would their frustration be expressed in disputes over authority? When Shackleton left, the health of some men had become alarming. The young Blackborow got his feet frozen and, while Shackleton was away, Macklin actually performed the amputation of the boy's toes in a makeshift operating room—under an overturned lifeboat.

Being the type of man he was, Shackleton drew on his last reserves of strength to rescue his people as soon as possible. He was ready to run almost any risk. What he did bordered on fearlessness. Had he, Crean and Worsley perished in crossing South Georgia, it was questionable whether Wild could have brought his group to Deception Island in the two stripped-down lifeboats remaining. In the final analysis, everything depended on the success of Shackleton's rescue mission.

In mountainous terrain, distance has little to do with travel time. Following a straight line, it was only about 30 miles to Stromness. But what would be waiting out there for the three men? How many ups and downs would they have to reckon with, how many detours would they have to make?

On May 19, 1916, they set out from Peggotty Camp at 0300 hours. The weather could not have been any better. The moon shone brightly and, for the first hour, showed them the way. Then a pea-soup fog rolled in.

On South Georgia, fog can be encountered in any season of the year and does not necessarily indicate deteriorating weather; but, in an area where the compass is not just helpful but essential, fog renders the traveler disoriented. Shackleton and his companions blundered toward a fjord on the island's north side, having mistaken Possession Bay for a great frozen lake. Only when the fog lifted did they realize their error. No whaling stations were at Possession Bay and it would have been impossible to walk along the coast from there. Having wasted precious time and energy, they had to climb back up and search for a way east along the snowy ridge.

For once, the spell of good weather continued—in fact, it lasted for the entire crossing. This saved their lives. They would not have survived a sudden drop in temperature or even another patch of fog. It is a break they richly deserved; even today the feats that Shackleton, Crean and Worsley performed seem superhuman. Overcoming all the technical terrain difficulties, they managed to cross South Georgia in a mere 36 hours. That meant making numerous detours, as they often had no idea of how the terrain looked on the far side of some ridge.

They crossed one of the region's most heavily-crevassed glaciers—one that now bears the name Tom Crean. Apparently, when they traversed, the glacier lay under a good snow covering, such that they hardly noticed the hidden crevasses. Perhaps the trio's most remarkable exploit, one that gives us some inkling of their plight, was "the sleigh ride." After repeated attempts, they finally found a way over one ridge. But the climbing had taken so much time that they could not get down into the valley before dark. That meant facing severe nocturnal cold at high altitude. Shackleton suggested to his comrades that they slide down the steep slope. He overruled all objections, as justifiable as they were. He knew that, unless they descended to a lower altitude, they would freeze to death.

Without further discussion, they coiled their climbing rope so that it became a kind of mat. Then, one behind the other, they got aboard: Shackleton in front, Crean wrapping his legs around him, and Worsley bringing up the rear. Without giving them time to consider the possible consequences of such a sleigh ride, Shackleton pushed off and, in the seconds that followed, they shot down the steep slope with the wind whistling in their ears. They knew nothing of what lay waiting down below—whether they would run headlong into a granite wall, or the snowy slope would change into a steep cliff over which they would plunge. Their chances of reaching the bottom of the slope alive were slight. But after a descent of over 2,000 feet in just a couple of minutes, the slope flattened out more and more, finally bringing the sleighing party up gently in a snow drift. Shackleton had again gambled with fate and won.

Night was falling, but they could see very well in the bright moonlight, so they went further. Except for brief stops to rest or cook some "hoosh" over the Primus, they kept on. Despite their exhaustion, they maintained an incredible pace. It should be remembered also that they were trekking through snow without skis or snowshoes, either of which would have made their crossing far easier.

At 6:30 on the next morning, standing on a steep slope, Shackleton heard what sounded like a steam whistle. Could it be the Stromness whaling station calling its men to work? If that was the case, Shackleton knew, the siren would blow again at 7:00 sharp. Breathlessly, the men started Worsley's chronometer. Precisely at 7:00 they heard the steam whistle again. They were on the right road, and this first sign of civilization summoned forth their last reserves of strength.

It would take until 1600 hours in the afternoon for the gaunt, exhausted men to surmount the last hurdles that stood on the way to Stromness. One of the workers at the Norwegian station, Mathias Andersen, was the first to spot the three scarecrows. He was shocked and rather angry that such filthy-looking individuals had been allowed onto the grounds of the whaling station. One of the three—Shackleton—asked hoarsely if he could lead them to the station's manager, Anton Andersen.

"Andersen isn't in Stromness any more," the worker replied. "Thoralf Sørlle runs the station now."

This was a stroke of luck, as Shackleton had met a man named Sørlle on his first visit with the ENDURANCE and had consulted with him at length.

"Good," he said, sighing with relief. "I know Sørlle."

The conversation that he had then with the whaling station manager has been described in the following terms:

In front of his house, Sørlle saw three filthy, ragged men and, in astonishment, asked them:

"Well?"

At this, Shackleton stepped forward and asked: "Don't you know me?"

The station manager replied, hesitantly, "I know your voice."

"My name is Shackleton."

The shock was such that the hard-bitten whaler had to turn away. He was crying. After the manager had regained his composure, he heard Shackleton ask:

"When did the war end?"

"The war hasn't ended," Sørlle said. "Millions have already been killed. Europe has gone mad, the whole world is crazy."

On April 24, they had set out in the JAMES CAIRD from Elephant Island to organize the rescue of their marooned companions. On May 20, they had reached Stromness, their goal. After Worsley left the following day for King Haakon Bay in the whaling vessel SAMSON to pick up Vincent, McCarthy and McNeish, the weather changed dramatically. If the storm, by then battering South Georgia, had overtaken Shackleton in the mountains hours earlier, he and his two comrades would have perished.

The SAMSON recovered not only the three other castaways but also the JAMES CAIRD and in this way, preserved her for posterity. Two more days would go by before the SAMSON, a sturdy whaling ship with powerful engines, could make her way back into Stromness, such was the ferocity of the storm. By then, Shackleton and Sørlle were hard at work hammering out a plan for rescuing the men marooned on Elephant Island.

After the epic boat journey and the crossing of South Georgia on foot, Shackleton had to deal with quite another kind of problem: the Admiralty rejected his appeal for help on behalf of the castaways in terms as icy as the coldest nights of his lifeboat journey.

14

Storm over South Georgia

On February 16, we are brought ashore in the inflatable dinghy. In the last few days, the weather has turned foul, so foul that we have had to change our anchorage several times. King Haakon Bay is not a terribly hospitable place. At the moment, the DAGMAR AAEN is lying behind sheltering Vincent Island with two bow lines carried ashore and an anchor out over the stern. The JAMES CAIRD II is moored alongside her.

Vincent, for whom the island is named, went through the JAMES CAIRD journey with Shackleton. Originally a North Sea trawler man, he joined the ENDURANCE expedition, a decision he was soon to regret. As with McNeish, Shackleton took Vincent along on the rescue mission to South Georgia because he regarded the man as pugnacious and rebellious. Under no circumstances would he leave him behind on Elephant Island, as he feared that Vincent could undermine the group. On the JAMES CAIRD Shackleton had him—and the carpenter—under control.

Unlike Shackleton, Crean and Worsley, we plan to take our time with the crossing. Aside from the fact that we plan to do filming, which involves packing a great deal of extra gear, this crossing takes on quite another meaning for us than it did for Shackleton. For us, it is not a matter of survival but of adventure. We worked very hard to bring the JAMES CAIRD II into King Haakon Bay. This trek over the island to Stromness represents the exact opposite of our punishing sea journey—you might say, we are rewarding ourselves.

Martin, Henryk and Torsten, who is coming along as our cameraman, have never before done any mountain climbing. For them, it is venturing into new territory, so naturally they are apprehensive. Sigga and I are there to guide the three of them safely over the crevasses of the glaciers. There's a first time for everyone, but we know they can do it.

A mountain of gear stands on the beach. There are five of us, so we need two tents, sleeping bags, stove, provisions, as well as full mountain climbing equipment. What a contrast with Shackleton's jury-rigged packs! In the end, each of our backpacks weighs 60 pounds—it's amazing how it all adds up. We take our time as Georg, Ralf and Tim are filming our preparations as well as our departure. Today we are going only a short distance in the direction of the glacier where we will camp overnight and then, the following morning, we will begin the actual crossing.

Driftwood, exactly as Worsley described it over 80 years ago, lies strewn all over the beach. In the age of sail, when countless windjammers went down in Cape Horn's storms, far more wreckage must have drifted through the

Southern Ocean. Even today, pieces of wooden boats, splintered planking, buoys from fishing nets, old shoes and other flotsam litter the beach in front of Peggotty Camp. The ocean currents go on unchanged. Nothing remains of the old camp itself; wind and wave have washed away any trace.

We have spent the last few days since arriving in King Haakon Bay resting and sorting through equipment for the crossing. Only now do we fully realize how tired and worn we are. The first day or two we have real problems with our walking. Our sense of balance is playing tricks on us—we keep trying to compensate for the motion of the heaving deck, only there isn't any motion here on the flat waters of the bay. We stumble and teeter on deck, hanging onto everything and struggling desperately to get our coordination back.

Our feet and ankles give us the most trouble. Still swollen, at times numb, they refuse to go into boots that fit perfectly before sailing. It will take weeks before the effects of the boat journey disappear completely. In other words, we look awfully peaked as we stand amid our hiking gear on the beach. Without meaning to, we now resemble Shackleton and his men. So we relish this chance to move, to see South Georgia's spectacular landscape and to experience nature. This crossing will even the score for the rugged voyage we've made.

Offshore, Martin, Sigga and Henryk had gone into raptures over the island's snowy landscape. "Just wait; that'll be our reward for the trip in JAMES CAIRD II," I kept promising them. And we all began clinging to this idea. That's why we were so determined to get into King Haakon Bay despite the storm and ice.

You may read all you want about Shackleton, but you get a much more vivid, personal impression by actually visiting the scene and grasping the subject directly than you can get by reading some journalist's work that's kept at a remove by geographical distance. A great deal of what we have experienced or will experience simply cannot be conveyed to readers, even with the best will and writing ability. Our experiences separate us from those who make judgments of Shackleton from their desk. We are as close to our predecessors as it is possible to get.

It is already late in the afternoon when we saddle up and start out slowly on our way. Today we plan to reach only the edge of the glacier, pull ourselves across the so-called Shackleton Gap, and camp there. We are moving through scree, so we must stay on the alert to avoid a slip. We trudge up the slope. In the scree fields not far from the glacier we find a fairly level patch with a tiny stream running through it. We pitch our two tents there while Ralf films us. Stirring our limbs has done us good, as one might work out a cramp. Though far from being back in shape, we have regained confidence in our legs and are starting to look at things calmly again. The first night in the tent, the gurgling of the brook and the intense fragrance that the land exudes—I sleep better than I have in weeks.

The next morning it takes us only minutes to reach the glacier. Sigga takes charge of Martin, Torsten and Henryk in traversing the glacier. Moving on crampons, using the ice-axe, roping up, safety techniques, rescue from crevasses—all that in a single crash course. That's how the first couple of hours are spent. The three are attentive pupils and Sigga presents her subject matter in a concise, lively fashion. After each student has gone through the practical exercises, we set out again.

The glacier is totally bare—there is no snow covering. All the crevasses gape open before us and we have no trouble spotting them—an advantage that turns all too quickly into a liability. On this easy terrain we are still all roped together; later we will split into two roped parties. Sigga leads, then come Martin, Henryk and Torsten, while I bring up the rear. Most of the time, just one long step takes us across the crevasses. Now and then Sigga backs off and looks for another crossing point. Our three mountaineering students do their best. Quickly, they gain confidence in themselves and in their equipment and, towards evening, we are working together as a team. We have reached the Shackleton Gap, the highest point on this glacier that flows into Possession Bay on the island's other side. It is one of the narrowest points on South Georgia. This is where Shackleton, Crean and Worsley had to climb back up, as they had mistaken the bay for a great lake. By the way, the name "Possession Bay" goes back to Captain James Cook who put into the bay and took possession of the island for Britain.

The weather abruptly deteriorates. Fog comes rolling up from the valley and before we know it, we are surrounded by thick swathes of cloud that reduce visibility to fifty yards. A strong, gusty wind blows. When we can no longer see the terrain lying ahead of us, we decide to camp. In this kind of country, orientation without visibility is difficult. Our only chart has a scale of 1:200,000 and is not particularly accurate. Pushing on, relying only on a compass bearing would surely lead us astray. That's because Worsley's map provides no course or bearing. They traveled only by sight—we want to follow their route, so we must proceed in exactly the same way. We keep peeking out of the tent to check on the weather. We need to orient ourselves or, at least, take a bearing but there's about as much visibility as inside a steam room—even the mountains right next to us disappear in the fog.

The weather shows signs of improving the next morning but no sooner do we get into our crampons than visibility worsens again. From here on, I lead. The terrain is very heavily crevassed and rather tricky in foggy weather. The one bearing I was able to take in the morning leads us only a short way in the right direction. In terrain so mountainous and with all contrast lost, we cannot make out more than a short stretch of ground ahead. Fog is the curse of this landscape.

Groping our way like drunkards, we negotiate the crevassed terrain, turning away here, seeking another path there. At noon, wind and rain start. In the hope that the fog may lift, we decide to pitch the larger "Expedition Dome" tent and wait one or two hours before pushing further on. We are incorrigible optimists.

From nowhere, a hurricane descends on us. In the next half-hour, we have a storm, the ferocity of which I have seldom experienced.

We lived through such violent storms in southern Patagonia, as well as on Greenland's east coast, and in the Aleutians. But I hardly remember such onslaughts of wind. At least, we have done the right thing instinctively—settling into our camp in time. It would have become impossible to set up a tent in this wind.

Five of us are huddled in a three-man tent, packed in like sardines. The gusts come roaring into us like an express train, smacking the tent with such force that two of us must brace our backs against the arched poles to keep them from snapping under the strain. Wind and snow drive the tent walls inward, leaving us with even less space than before. As night falls, the howl of the storm becomes so ear-splitting that we can barely make ourselves understood. We abandon immediately the idea of pitching a second tent, for it would just be blown to ribbons in a fraction of a second. No, we have to stick it out, as cramped and uncomfortable as we may be.

"So this is the reward you promised us," Henryk yells over the angry flapping of the nylon fabric.

"And we actually believed you. We were all so happy about the nice, quiet hike—no more being wet or cold, no more storms," Martin adds, smiling.

Sigga rushes to defend me: "Come, now, we're on dry land. We can't drown or be dashed against rocky cliffs or run into an iceberg. At the worst, it's a little discomfort."

Despite the miserable situation, we have to laugh. As uncomfortable as it is, this stormy night cannot be compared to stormy nights aboard the JAMES CAIRD II.

Nevertheless, the night is terribly unpleasant. Packed in on top of each other, unable to budge one inch, we remain in twisted positions, praying for the night to end and the storm to subside. The initial blizzard now turns into a true rainstorm. We can moan all we want, but the next morning there is not a piece of equipment that is remotely dry. Stiff, we wriggle out of our sleeping-bags at daybreak and wait for the storm to abate. Late in the morning the weather finally settles down sufficiently so we can think about pushing on, but the actual conditions are far from promising. It keeps on raining and the visibility is so poor that we can only see the crevasses when they are two feet away from us. Torsten tries desperately to take some decent pictures but as soon as he gets the cap off a film of water spreads over the lens.

Henryk mutters, "Damn weather!" Undaunted, though, he keeps moving. We are all terribly cold again. Mainly, our feet suffer. Our leather boots are sodden from the interminable rain. Water sloshes around inside, getting between our toes. The circulation in our lower extremities is still not what it should be. My feet are ice cold and they hurt. To top it off, they are still swollen; my boots become too tight. That evening, the nails on both big toes turn purple—I will lose them at the end of the journey.

While the storm redoubles its violence, we climb up to a gap to reach the opposite side. We are panting from our exertions as we finally reach the top where the wind hits us with jackhammer force. Though I wear crampons, carry a 60-pound backpack, use two ski-poles for support and, at 165 pounds, am not exactly a flyweight, a gust sends me flying. I do a forward somersault, landing hard in the scree twenty feet below, a tangle of limbs.

While I sit there, slightly dazed, sorting out my arms and legs, I see Torsten take a nasty spill. The wind swoops through the gap with fighter-jet speeds. Though we go roped together, it knocks us off our feet time after time. Whenever we sense a particularly strong gust coming, we crouch down and wait till it's over. South Georgia is certainly not showing us its sunny side. With no equipment and in weather like this, Shackleton, Crean and Worsley wouldn't have stood a chance.

When we put the gap behind us, the wind—but not the interminable rain—dies down. Somewhere up ahead, in the rain and fog, lies another chain of mountains that must be crossed. It is impossible in this weather. With great effort, we manage to pitch the tent in the lee of an ice fault and, drenched as we are, crawl inside. Our feet look the way our hands looked on the JAMES CAIRD II: dead-white, ice-cold and shriveled like prunes. Life returns after we have the Primus stove going and have devoured our freeze-dried potato stew along with pemmican and BP5 cookies. Henryk conjures up a hip-flask of vodka from which all of us—except Martin, the teetotaler—take a healthy slug. What a difference the thin nylon fabric of the tent makes. It keeps wind and rain out, it stores up the warmth of the stove (as long as it burns), and gives us the coziness of a family home. We drink hot tea and joke about our predicament. The others can't get over my somersault—purely involuntary, though seemingly acrobatic.

"You still could do a little work on the stance and, particularly, the landing," Sigga says. "With a bit more experience, your somersaults would be quite acceptable."

The next morning, the weather finally improves. Fog still hangs over the glacier, but the sun is coming out. Best of all, the wind and rain have stopped. All the same, it takes will power to get back into our wet clothing and soggy boots. While we are striking camp, the sun breaks through and the fog lifts. For the first time in three days we can get the lay of the land.

The view is sensational. To our left is the open ocean with Antarctic Bay and, high above us, abrupt mountain peaks.

Under normal weather conditions, we could have done this distance in a few hours—even with all our stuff. Thus far, the terrain problems have not been too bad. Weather is the decisive factor. Certainly, Shackleton, Worsley and Crean did the right thing by taking advantage of the good weather and pressing on as fast as possible.

Ahead of us, clearly visible in the sunshine, lies the knife-edged ridge from which the three of them—in complete darkness—went plunging down, using a rope mat as a makeshift sled.

The problem is simple: Several passes lead through the great ridges. But who knows what kind of descent is waiting on the other side? Nobody knew in 1916, as no man had ever set foot up there. They tried the pass furthest to the right, reaching its saddle only to find a steep icy slope on the other side. Making their way down would be impossible. Tired, bitterly disappointed, they turned and climbed to the saddle of the next gap—and once more they found a sheer couloir that they could not descend. Meanwhile, their steep ascent had all but exhausted them. There was no time to lose. At the third pass they were in luck. The descent did seem feasible. By now it was already late in the afternoon. Shackleton feared that, at this elevation and in their exhausted state, they would freeze to death. The men had to be utterly desperate to let themselves in for such a wild sleigh ride.

Reaching the cornice in question, we are greeted by a spectacular sight. Below us, the Crean Glacier, as heavily crevassed as any glacier can be. On either side, the dark bands of the moraine; snow- and ice-draped summits; further east *Nunatak*, a rocky peak jutting from the ice that we will pass on our route. The snow slope in front of us drops off steeply. Under favorable conditions, it would make an ideal run on skis. The party of three men in 1916 were neither inclined to consider such an idea nor equipped with skis. They had only a coil of rope as makeshift sled. Wild horses couldn't make me go sleigh riding down the slope on our rope—unless I were as desperate as our predecessors.

This year there is very little snow. We are carrying Snow Trekkers—short skis—that served us well in the few snowfields we have crossed thus far. We cannot ski on this particular slope just now, so we descend carefully with our crampons. For Martin, Henryk and Torsten, this is the steepest slope they have ever done. Deliberately, with great concentration, they set one cramponed boot in front of the other, bracing themselves with their ice-axes and grimly plodding along behind me. They do this very well. At the bottom of the slope run the ridges of a moraine. We drop our backpacks and look back. We have descended about 1500 feet. Before us lies the Crean Glacier with its labyrinth of crevasses. Judging by what we can see, it will not be easy to find a way through. The glacier is totally denuded of snow. Except for a few remnants, the crevasses themselves are clear of snow, permitting an unimpeded view into their depths. Winter is undoubtedly the best season for a crossing, as the enormous snowfall plugs the crevasses, making them passable. Shackleton, Crean and Worsley moved over the glacier in a straight line— for us, an impossibility.

We push ahead rapidly until the first and second middle moraines. Then the crevasses yawn wider and wider. Sigga and I go on to scout the way while the other three wait for us. The first route we try leads us into a deadend. The crevasses are so wide that it becomes impossible to cross. We try another spot—with exactly the same result. We have used up so much time that we are ready to camp again. To the south, the Wilckens Peaks tower over us. I feel rather downcast because I haven't managed to find a way over the glacier.

The next morning we do it. Turn and twist as we may, the terrain remains very difficult; this is a slow, arduous descent. Henryk, Torsten and Martin demonstrate great skill: To see them, you would never believe it was their first time out on crampons.

Finally, we leave the valley and, with it, the Crean Glacier, the most formidable leg of the entire crossing. Our three predecessors were far less aware of its difficulties than we are. Was it because the glacier wasn't so heavily crevassed in those days? I doubt it. Even though South Georgia's glaciers are subject to continual change, the terrain was deeply fissured even back then. I think it is more likely that the enormous quantities of snow forced in by the wind created a relatively strong underlayer. Perhaps without suspecting it, they were trekking from one snow bridge to the next. Even if they had known about this, they would not have been able to change their tactics very much—they'd been on their feet continuously since leaving Peggotty Camp.

Above the valley, through which the Crean Glacier runs, we stumble across the wreckage of a helicopter. Lying upside down, its cockpit is completely buried in snow. The rotors lie strewn about. It is a grisly reminder of the Falklands War of 1982. During a gale, the Royal Marines chopper made a crash landing. From what we later learned, they all escaped unharmed. The rescue helicopter also had to make a forced landing and it wasn't until the third one that the survivors could be picked up. The wreck has been lying on the ice ever since.

Finally, we pass *Nunatak*, the peak sighted before our descent onto the Crean Glacier that runs straight to Fortuna Glacier. The weather has at last come to terms with us and grants us the most lovely sunshine. It is windless, so our wet clothing quickly dries and life is again wonderful. We camp in the middle of Fortuna Glacier, sunning ourselves and drying out our gear. Afterwards, I set up the antenna of our short-wave radio and try to contact the DAGMAR AAEN.

15

Glaciers and Penguins

D elta India X-ray X-ray—this is Delta India X-ray X-ray Mobile."

Crackling and static in the loudspeaker and then Karsten's voice breaks through. In this age of cellular and satellite phones, the slightly distorted radio transmission has something touchingly nostalgic about it. The shortwave sets are reliable. In this remote corner of the globe, that justifies their existence.

"We're waiting for you at the Stromness whaling station with the two boats. How are you doing? Did you manage with that storm all right? How does everything look up there?"

Karsten seems relieved to hear me. Apparently the weather hit them hard, too.

On the day after we began our crossing, the DAGMAR AAEN sailed for Camp Cove. That's the place where Shackleton and his five companions first landed on South Georgia. Our friends took the inflatable dinghy as far as the beach, but then that was it. The narrow coastal strip was packed with fur seals who gave the intruders a loud, angry greeting. The message was clear: "Beat it! This is our territory!" A landing was quite out of the question. Karsten and his people bowed to superior force.

While Katja—with an occasional change of company—sailed JAMES CAIRD II along the coast following DAGMAR AAEN, the weather began deteriorating slowly but steadily. To be on the safe side, Karsten sent a towline aboard the JAMES CAIRD II and hurried through Stewart Strait trying to make the island's sheltered north coast.

On the afternoon of February 18, in threatening weather, they attempted to anchor in Right Whale Bay. At 1600 hours the logbook recorded 25-knot winds. By 1700 hours the winds were already at 40 knots and a bit later were blowing with hurricane force at 70 knots. Naturally, no anchor would hold in that storm. They tacked back and forth the whole night, searching for a bit of cover from the land. Meanwhile, astern of the DAGMAR AAEN, the crewless, orphaned JAMES CAIRD pitched and tossed at the end of a long line.

If the cutter's crew had a hurricane down there in the fjord, under the lee of the land, how much worse must the storm have raged up on the plateau where we stuck it out, five in one tent. The crew had good reason to be worried about us. It becomes all the more important that we have made radio contact today.

"There's a mooring buoy off Stromness for research vessels. It is not occupied at the moment, so we've made fast to it." For the first time in a long while, the crew of DAGMAR AAEN can sleep peacefully.

The next morning begins the way the previous evening finished—sunshine, apparently unlimited visibility, calm and warmth. It's marvelous. We slowly descend Fortuna Glacier until at last we reach the chain of mountains stretching behind Fortuna Bay. Shackleton, Crean and Worsley mistook this fjord for Stromness Bay and trekked over the glacier in the direction of the open sea. At some point they realized that there was no glacier at Stromness and that it must in fact be Fortuna Bay. In their state of exhaustion, the setback must have been horrendous.

The descent to Fortuna Bay over a slope covered with scree and loose rock demands all our concentration. With good reason, Worsley referred to the place as Heartbreak Ridge.

There, they left behind their Primus stove, as they had run out of fuel. Seeing the first clump of tussock grass before us, we know that we are definitely done with the ice. On the beach fur seals and elephant seals bask in the sun and the curious king penguins strut around. It seems like paradise to us. While Martin makes polite conversation with his flippered friends, we drop our packs onto the sand. Boots are pulled off. With feet and heads resting on a clump of grass, we doze off blissfully. All of South Georgia's savage beauty lies before us. An idyllic place for the suckling of young seals and penguins—if the weather were always this mild.

We have long since forgotten how it feels to be wet, cold, seasick. We are in another world, at peace with our surroundings. We still haven't made Stromness, but that will come. Somehow, for me, the crossing seems to end right here and now. It is the great contrast, the paradise regained within myself, I am at one with myself, with my friends, with my surroundings, with the expedition—with everything.

We set out again, but now it is a stroll rather than a hike. Torsten has found his photographic heaven with the king penguins. In fact, none of us can see enough of these creatures which, though somewhat smaller than emperor penguins, strike us as being more attractive and having a truly regal air. When Torsten sets his video camera on the sand, several penguins make straight for it. Curious, they study the strange machine close up, nudging it with their beaks, considering it from every angle, as if they knew exactly what it was for.

In another place, elephant seals block our way. Unlike the quick fur seals, these merely bellow and pant indignantly but, even as they make these threats, their eyes close again, their heads landing with a dull thud in the sand and the din of their snoring begins anew. We climb over grassy hillocks and see giant stormy petrels on the beach waiting for prey, watching as the king penguins pass majestically, off for a swim. The penguins don't walk, they don't waddle—they strut, and then, like a shot, dive into the water.

Since Shackleton's days, the König Glacier has apparently retreated a mile or more. To reach the other side, we have to walk around the entire estuary of the fjord. It is difficult as torrents of water from the melting glacial snow and ice cut deep, impassable gullies in the earth. We struggle to find a way through these rivers, but the water is too deep and swift for us to cross. But nothing can yank us from our inner and outer serenity. Somehow, we like the idea of not being able to reach Stromness today. We gladly put off the river crossing till tomorrow, preferring to stop and look for a nice campsite. We find a green meadow overlooking a pool of crystal clear water. Henryk starts by pulling off his boots; then he goes traipsing barefoot through the grass. "I've waited a long time for this," he says, enraptured. "This is the greatest!"

With great relish, we eat our last reserves, leaving only enough for tomorrow's breakfast. We can make out the saddle in the ridge separating us from Stromness. Our route for tomorrow's climb is clear. Aside from the fact that we have to do a good bit of climbing, no further difficulties lie ahead.

Today this valley gives us our reward for the hardships we have endured. We drink one cup of tea after the other—and talk. Sigga, Henryk, Martin and Torsten comment on the ocean passage and the crossing on foot and I am fascinated by their different views.

"The storm on the glacier the first day of the crossing terrified me. That was where I learned that being on land didn't mean being safe. I kept thinking that the tent could blow apart, the fuel for the stove might run out, and we would be at the mercy of the storm, the rain, and the cold," Henryk says.

Martin finds the crossing a real challenge. "The hardest part was going down the steep scree slope to Fortuna Bay. Our boots skidded on the round stones. I didn't really care for those long steps we took over the crevasses. But the cold in my hands and feet was what I found worst of all," he continues. "Especially that morning after the storm on the ice when I had to put on my frozen boots and those cold, wet hats I used for gloves because mine had shrunk."

Sigga and I regarded the stormy night as just one more uncomfortable and unpleasant situation rather than a real threat. We'd both been through many such nights while for Martin and Henryk this was their first time in a bad storm on land. There is a delightful anecdote about Captain John C. Voss whose Northwest Indian dugout canoe TILLIKUM rode out a typhoon. Lying hove-to, making himself comfortable below, he lit up a cigar, and thought about "the poor souls on land." Whether this is fact or fiction remains an open question, but certainly things we don't know always seem much more threatening than what's familiar. If someone who has never driven a car were thrust into the rush-hour traffic of a big city, he would almost certainly die of fright.

Torsten is enthusiastic about the crossing. "All those different kinds of terrain! I had never dreamt there were so many techniques for climbing and trekking. Hiking through scree or with crampons is totally unlike skiing or climbing steep slopes. Simply thrilling. And the way the weather continually changed—from a hurricane to a dead calm!"

We discuss the fact that there are many people who do not understand the point of this expedition. We are constantly asked that old question: "What use is this to anyone?" as if the legitimacy of such a voyage depended on some lofty purpose. But then how much human endeavor serves a useful purpose? Fridtjof Nansen once said: "Life has no point. There is nothing in nature that could be termed a point. *Point* is a purely human idea."

Martin tells us a joke:

"The U.N. is holding a contest for all its member states. The countries still left in the final round are France, England, America and Germany. The assignment: write a book about elephants. At the deadline, the French submit a charming, splendidly illustrated book under the title *L'Amour des Ele-*

phants. The British have also produced a deluxe leatherbound book. Its title: *How to Chase an Elephant.* The Americans enter with a paperback book entitled *Elephants—How to Make Them Bigger and Better.* The German delegation publishes a rather modest edition. Title: *A Brief Introduction to the Study of Elephants, 12 Volumes.*"

We get a good laugh out of this exaggerated reflection of the German mind. What would life be if it were always judged in practical terms and with the mentality of a bookkeeper? Without dreams and vision, we stagnate and die. We must allow them. "Happy are those who dream dreams and are willing to pay the price to make them come true." That holds true for all areas of life. The quality of life resides precisely in the individual's inventiveness and creativity. Dreams are the spice of life, whatever their nature. They inspire vision, awaken creativity. And this also applies to any business concern. The young creators of the New Economy are very successful examples of this. While our corporations are stifled by bureaucracy, these men and women use totally unconventional methods and, suddenly, the German economy isn't doing so badly. These young people don't whine and complain. Being dynamic, making something out of one's time—that's their credo. It is useful and it makes sense. In my opinion, the way we spend our lives is legitimate as long as what we do does not harm anyone. If our dreams can even inspire others, that's even better.

The next morning brings us back once more to the harsh reality of our routine. The crossing of the glacial river proves more difficult than we have anticipated. For a solid hour we slog through mud, sand and scree. At last, we find a kind of delta where the river branches out and the current slackens. Nonetheless, the crossing is difficult. I pull off my trousers, secure myself to the climbing rope and wade in. The river is coming from the edge of the glacier only a few hundred yards away, so the water is freezing. The bottom is so marshy that, with every step, I sink thigh-deep. Between the swift current and the icy water I begin to feel a little faint. Now the water is up to my hips. As I finally clamber up onto the other bank, my legs ache with cold. I dance around like Rumpelstiltskin, trying to get the circulation back in my legs. One after another, the others ford the glacial tributary, and one after another, they too dance around to warm their legs.

Fifty yards further, there's another arm of the river to ford. Martin strays off the route, loses his footing and nearly goes plunging headlong in the water. He manages to recover and pulls himself back onto the bank, but now he is half-frozen. Though shaken by the experience, he tries to cross again. This time he sticks to the route and reaches the far bank on legs stiff with cold. In spite of everything, Torsten goes on filming and photographing while Henryk curses again in Polish (giving me strict orders not to quote him). Sigga is considerably shorter than us and the glacial water comes up to her navel. As always, she accepts every hardship with stoicism and a smile on her face.

The river was nothing like this in Shackleton's time. For one thing, being winter then, it must have been considerably colder, so any streams running from the glacier were little more than rivulets. For another thing, the glacier was larger and longer in those days; in all likelihood, they were able to cross dry-shod.

The fine silt sticks all over our feet and legs. Before

putting away our rope for good and climbing the last slope before Stromness, we bask in the warmth of the sun for a moment. Once more it almost seems like bidding farewell to a great adventure.

Finally we see the pond where Crean crashed through the ice and then, thoroughly drenched, had to keep on going. I stand there for a moment, look back and then follow Sigga, who is already hurrying on ahead. Minutes later the crest of the ridge looms up before us. It is covered with steep scree slopes. Shackleton, Crean and Worsley almost descended the fall line and therefore still had a hair-raising rappel down a waterfall. There is an easy descent a little further left. They simply wanted to get down and, in their exhausted, desperate state, chose the more difficult, more dangerous and, in terms of time, longer way. We take the easier, safer route.

In a few minutes, we can see the bay, with the tiny DAG-MAR AAEN and, ashore, the ruins of the old Stromness whaling station. As we stand there for a minute or two, looking at the scenery, familiar voices reach our ears. Ralf, Georg and Tim have come rushing up the mountain with all their equipment to film our descent and accompany us over the last mile or two. From the natural way our three friends move over this terrain, you would think they had never done anything else. Together, we go down the slope. The hills around us become green. Happily, we trudge over moss that grows along the course of a stream, finally passing our first fur seals that give their usual, unfriendly greeting. We are descending the same trail that Shackleton, Crean and Worsley must have taken to reach the station in 1916. Georg shows us the way to the house of former station manager Sørlle. We remain standing in front of the building, setting down our packs and looking around, a bit sadly.

A plaque explains the significance of this house. Can tourists visiting the old station and seeing the plaque fathom what those three men went through? What it means to sail from Antarctica to South Georgia in a 22-foot boat? What courage, what desperation, and what superhuman determination they needed and, finally, what skill and knowledge was required, not merely to survive, but to make their landfall? Though what we have done is not the same, we have nonetheless come very close to those events—at any rate, closer than anyone else.

Epilogue

Grytviken is the best known of the old South Georgia whaling stations. There on Cumberland Bay are also the headquarters of a British garrison. Since the Falklands War of 1982 there has been a military presence on this remote island. The base is situated at King Edward Point rather a distance from the old whaling station that, like Stromness, can be recognized from afar by its rusting tanks, windswept buildings, and bleached skeletons of wooden structures. Two half-sunk whaling vessels lie at a rotting pier and, at another pier a little further on, there is a third. Next to it is CURLEW, the sailboat belonging to Tim and Pauline Carr who dropped anchor here seven years ago and who now live permanently on South Georgia.

Before our expedition, Tim and Pauline had e-mailed us valuable information and tips about South Georgia. I am eager to make their acquaintance. Standing on the decrepit pier as we come in dead slow with DAGMAR AAEN, the couple receive our docking lines. JAMES CAIRD II, which Karsten, Uschi, Katja and Ute are sailing from Stromness to Grytviken, will not make port until later. For such a desolate station, there are an awful lot of people waiting for us. Besides Tim and Pauline, Pat Lucock and his wife Sarah as well as some of their friends are there. In other words, the whole population of Grytviken has turned out—there may be as many as seven in the crowd. We hear applause when the DAGMAR AAEN is finally made fast.

Though we have never met, we are welcomed like old friends. A bottle of champagne lovingly ornamented with postage stamps featuring the Shackleton motif, a good luck card and many a cheery shout of "Welcome" and "Congratulations." These expressions of affection are touching; the gesture convinces us at last that our expedition is over—and is crowned with success. Pat Lucock comes aboard. The marine officer responsible for passport and Customs, Pat is also harbormaster. We go through the formalities quickly. We have now officially entered—our great adventure has come to a close. In a few days the HANSEATIC will make port and take the JAMES CAIRD II aboard and bring her back to Hamburg. Over and out, back to normalcy.

Wash, put on clean duds, trim fingernails, cut beard, comb hair, lie in the sun, write postcards. All of us know the feeling at the end of an expedition. The sudden calm, the release of tension, loafing—but also a certain emptiness. Something is missing, something of what we gladly put behind us, yet that we miss all the same. It's crazy. I have seldom been through such a harrowing experience. Being cold and wet, knowing fear and fatigue, living in such a cramped space. The musty odor of the cabin, the pangs of conscience over something left undone at home. Was all that worth it? I have known the answer for quite some time.

Would I set out again on some other expedition? I wouldn't want to repeat the same adventure but, yes, something else, something equally challenging. Making dreams come true. Giving in to restlessness, allowing curiosity and intuition to take you into a new phase of your life. For me, dreams are the driving force; they are meaningful and worth the risk every time. What we do may not please everyone. However those very people who admonish, point their fingers, reproaching us for the uselessness and irresponsibility of our actions, are often not well-intentioned. I see this again and again.

In personal conversations with people from well-known magazines and production firms, I am challenged to give up such aids as GPS or other vital electronic equipment which now costs so little. These same folks who make these challenges have nothing against using satellite communications—naturally, they intend to keep themselves up to date. These are often the same people who, when something goes wrong, are always there to crow: "That's just what we've been saying all along!"

As I enter the Grytviken cemetery that same evening, it feels like a windless summer day. A row of wooden crosses date, for the most part, back to whaling times which lasted here well into the 1960s. At the far end of the small burial ground rises a rough-hewn granite stone with a few memorial plaques in front of it. This is the grave of Sir Ernest Shackleton.

His story does not end with the arrival in Stromness. The 22 castaways on Elephant Island were still waiting—and a further ten at McMurdo Sound, who still believed that Shackleton and his team would be coming through for them. The weight of his responsibilities remained; the incredible boat journey and the crossing had left their mark on him: he seemed changed.

On a large seal-hunting ship, SOUTHERN SKY, the boilers were fired up. On May 23, exactly one month after his start from Elephant Island and only three days after arriving in Stromness, he left South Georgia with Crean and Worsley aboard the whaling ship to rescue the men marooned on Elephant Island. McNeish, Vincent and McCarthy were able to get passage on another ship bound for England. They were never again to meet. Just three weeks after his return to England, Tim McCarthy was killed in action.

Shortly before the SOUTHERN SKY sailed, the men were again invited to a reception aboard the ORWELL. Aside from Shackleton and his companions, among the guests were a number of old Norwegian whalers some of whom had fished these waters for as long as 40 years. One of these men gave a brief speech: "I know the Southern Ocean quite well and never heard of such a wonderful feat of seamanship as bringing a 22-foot lifeboat from Elephant Island to South Georgia, and, to top it off, they trekked across the snow and ice of the island's mountainous interior. I consider it an honor to shake the hand of Sir Ernest and his comrades."

Their recognition meant more to Shackleton than all the praise in the world. These were men who spoke his language, men cast from the same mold. Here on South Georgia he was still living in the time capsule that had surrounded him and his men since leaving England. Now all that would change. The war that still raged had altered the world in every respect. The front pages of the newspapers were full of war news; hardly anyone took notice of the relatively insignificant drama being played out in the Polar Sea. A few castaways meant little indeed when weighed against the drama of the worldwide conflict.

When he returned to the Falklands without achieving anything because of ice off Elephant Island, virtually nobody in Port Stanley took notice. On the contrary, he was being reproached for shirking his duty at the front. "Adventurer Plays in Polar Sea," said the press. That same day, while the *Times* ran a brief article titled "Shackleton's Men Rescued at Fourth Attempt," its front page carried a roster of 4,530 British soldiers killed, wounded or missing.

The Admiralty proved anything but friendly. After considerable hemming and hawing, they did agree to send help, but also insisted on taking charge of the rescue operation themselves—apparently for the purpose of humiliating Shackleton.

Shackleton wouldn't have been the man he was had he left the fate of his men to some timid government official. He talked the government of Uruguay into lending him a decrepit old survey-ship, the Pesca No. 1, for the trip to Elephant Island. That attempt also failed in the ice. He made his next try with the 70-foot schooner Emma. Aboard this sailing vessel, Worsley was in his element. But the small, 40-year-old schooner simply could not break through the belt of ice to reach the castaways.

Shackleton, by now in Punta Arenas, was nearly desperate. He drank more than was good for him and grew taciturn. The Chilean government finally made the sea-going tug Yelcho available to him, so that another attempt could be made.

This time luck was on his side. On August 30, a good four months after JAMES CAIRD had sailed from Elephant Island, YELCHO reached Point Wild. Without wasting a minute, Sir Ernest rowed ashore to pick up his men. Shackleton had arrived just in time to rescue them. He did not even take the time to inspect the improvements they had made in the camp, of which they were justly proud; he wanted only to get going before the ice closed in.

After a triumphal reception in Puntas Arenas, he cabled his wife Emily: "I have done it. Damn the Admiralty. I wonder who is responsible for their attitude to me. Not a life lost and we have been through hell. Soon I will be home and then I will rest."

It would be some time before he had that well-earned rest. In Australia and New Zealand, where he went next to organize the relief of the Ross Sea group, he was met by a wave of rejection and hostility. Here, too, the war had left its scars. As usual, Shackleton had no money; mounting debts and the self-promotion of former members of the expedition threatened to bring the rescue of the Ross Sea party to a degrading conclusion.

Shackleton, relieved of the command of his ship AURORA, sailed in her as a passenger. On arriving in the Ross Sea, he would learn that three of his men had lost their lives in the course of the expedition and that the survivors looked even more wretched than the men marooned on Elephant Island. Describing the experiences of this group would fill another book. The AURORA group's sufferings—and the deaths of three of its members—were utterly unnecessary. This must have had a shattering effect on everyone and, most of all, on Shackleton, for whom the well-being of his men was something sacred. Men had died albeit not when they were under his direct command.

Back in England, Shackleton lost his grip more and more. He smoked and drank excessively. Overweight, he was plagued with coughs and infections. He was losing his indomitable spirit. Even his private life was coming apart at the seams. He rarely spent time any longer with his wife Emily; increasingly, he saw other women, a couple of whom were actually paying his bills, as he himself had next to no money. The world to which he had returned was no longer his.

Shackleton organized one last expedition, which took its name from the ship QUEST. It was an escape more than anything. The goals and tasks for the expedition were muddled, basically unclear, but that wasn't the point.

In September 1921, the QUEST sailed from England bound south for Antarctica even though plans had been made for going to the Arctic. It did not matter. Shackleton and several old companions meant to get away, to revisit a life and a time they were familiar with. On the journey south Shackleton suffered a first, severe heart attack; he recovered nonetheless, and refused to allow the surgeon to run any tests on him. Early January 1921 the QUEST reached South Georgia. There, he was at home—not in England from which he had become alienated.

They passed Possession Bay, Fortuna Bay; once again seeing old landmarks that remained graven in their minds since their crossing of the island. Many of the whalers were already waiting for them in Grytviken. It was a reunion of old friends. They walked over the green slopes of the mountains and soon Shackleton became himself again. Only Macklin, the surgeon and long-standing companion of Shackleton, was worried. On the evening of January 5, he was summoned to Shackleton's cabin. The Boss had suffered another attack. That conversation would be the last between the two. Macklin is said to have warned Shackleton to change his lifestyle.

"You're always after me to give something up. What am I supposed to give up now?" was Shackleton's question.

"Alcohol, Boss. I don't think it agrees with you," came Macklin's answer. Within the hour, Shackleton died. At his wife's request, he was buried in the Grytviken cemetery among the whalers and seafarers to whom he had always felt much closer than anyone in the so-called civilized world.

How would the men of the QUEST proceed now without the Boss? His closest friend, Frank Wild, carried the expedition to its conclusion—at least, as he saw it. Even in death, Shackleton's charisma held the crew together. After their return, the men scattered all over the world. The end of an era had come.

Was Shackleton now the unlucky hero, the eternal second? Many contemporaries saw it that way. It took none other than Amundsen to set the picture straight: "Don't let it be said that Shackleton has failed. No man fails who sets an example of high courage, of unbroken resolution, of unshrinking endurance."

While Scott went down in the annals of history as the tragic national hero, Shackleton became a legend even in his own lifetime—a man full of contradictions and dreams who never truly attained his expedition goals but who possessed the gift for inspiring others. Scott stood for endurance and sacrifice in the name of duty. That was the stuff heroes were made of in those days. In my opinion, Shackleton looms incomparably larger than Scott, the tragic hero. Wiser—albeit a poor planner—Shackleton demonstrated greater prudence, a greater gift for improvisation and a boundless will to survive. He was a positive figure who possessed a sense of responsibility. What Scott lacked was the human dimension, something that Shackleton embodies like no one else.

Thankfully, I live in another world. I am tremendously fascinated by the stories of the great discoveries and, in particular, by the human aspect. Still I wouldn't want to have lived in those days. Over the years I have become a seafarer and polar explorer of the old breed—but without having to share their drama. I am free, a traveler between worlds, one who can always take a few steps back to get a better view. Again and again, I cross over the border from tranquil, civilized life to the hard, real and—occasionally—dangerous life of the explorers. There's nothing left to conquer—aside from ourselves or knowledge. We need these myths for they give rise to dreams and these dreams prompt us to act. I seek not to debunk myths but, simply, to see what lies behind them.

Truly plunging into a legend, reliving a historic journey involves reading reports of those expeditions. Those reports are tremendously enlightening. They are contemporary documents that put straight so many wrong ideas, and prompt reflection.

The expeditions of earlier times are part of our history, our culture. A kind of time capsule, they give us a glimpse into the longings of people, into the moral concepts of the past. The story of exploration also provides insights into leadership ability, crisis management, into team-building methods—concepts whose relevance remains unchanged.

Certainly, modern polar exploration is efficient, but it is

also sterile. Exploring in a super-reinforced icebreaker or a 400-foot long containership seems as daring as a bus ride across town. Today's adventurers rely on technology that has become routine. They move the levers but no longer determine their own fate.

The polar regions represent border zones, limits. They are the ends of the earth and form an interface between earth and space—simply because of their extreme environment. There, space and time are lost in infinity. Light and dark, warmth and cold are like life and death. In this respect nothing has changed since Shackleton's day.

"You know, Arved, South Georgia is my dreamland," Sigga told me. "The terrain offers simply everything. It doesn't give anything away, but those who have earned it come away with the experience of a lifetime.

"Every time one of you grumbled about having cold fingers made me angry on the voyage," she went on. "You seemed to lack respect for this place. Should people complain about cold hands here, in a place that offers such sensations and experiences?

"I'm making this journey because it teaches me that our horizons can always be expanded. We run into limits in every aspect of life—in human interaction, for example. We have to consider the other person; we learn to speak our minds without having a closed mind to what others say. And then there are physical boundaries: You think you can't go another step, and then you keep going another couple of hours or you steer for the whole watch, even if it seems endless. Almost anything is possible—if you really want to do it. I saw it here more clearly than ever before."

Appendix

The Rig of the JAMES CAIRD II

Searching the Literature

I have searched the literature for any references to boats like the JAMES CAIRD, a lifeboat of the ENDURANCE. With her double-ended design, she resembles a whaleboat, a boat of Scandinavian origin—say, for example, from the Faroes Islands. There are many photographs of her being rowed, but very few showing her under sail. The masts and sails of lifeboats were customarily lashed to the thwarts, the sails being set only when necessary.

In her book, *The Endurance,* Caroline Alexander reports that no photos of the sailing rig exist for the *Caird.* It was probably a simple gaff rig. From the photos in the book, it has been possible to work out the position and length of the masts. *Shackleton's Boat Journey,* the book written by Frank Worsley, skipper of the ENDURANCE, refers to a standing lug as opposed to a dipping lug for the mainmast. Unlike a dipping lug, a standing lugsail need not be shifted around the mast when changing tacks. The other sails were probably a jib and a small mizzen. Exact records do not exist because the sails for the JAMES CAIRD were taken from all three lifeboats in a mix-and-match fashion, and may not have represented the standards of the time.

In the book *Bemastung und Takelung der Schiffe des 18. Jahrhunderts* by F.L. Middendorf, simple formulas are given for typical measurements for masts and spars for the respective rigs. *The Sailmaker's Apprentice* by Emiliano Marino provides very helpful information about lugsails. Material on lug rigs can also be found in *Seemannschaft: Handbuch für den Yachtsport.* Actually, this rig is still seen on the small cutters being sailed in German youth sailing programs.

My research did not lead to a single clear rigging or sail plan but, rather, to numerous references to possible designs. The rigging and sail plans for the JAMES CAIRD replica were re-designed and re-sized for authenticity and also with keeping in mind the cold and stormy Antarctic Ocean. The main requirements were safety (even adventurers like to come home alive), efficiency (a fast trip), and ease of handling.

The Sails

A major problem with the JAMES CAIRD was her strong weather helm which had to be offset by constant counter-rudder. This slowed her down and impeded her ability to maneuver. The problem is characteristic of luggers without bowsprit.

The basic sail plan of JAMES CAIRD II consists of mizzen, mainsail, and jib. In addition, a storm jib is provided for heavy weather. All sails in the basic plan can be reefed. The reef points are aligned with the clews so that the jib leads do not have to be re-adjusted (advantage in handling). The main sheet is led to the mizzen chainplates (no additional fittings are required; besides, chainplates are a very solid attachment). For the jib, a padeye is provided.

For the sailcloth, there was a choice of cotton, Duradon and Dacron. Cotton would be authentic but it has drawbacks: it needs to be broken in, tends to become stiff when wet, and is subject to mildew. Also it could not be supplied in the desired tan color. Dacron, standard today with cruising sailboats, offered many advantages. Unfortunately, it isn't authentic. As a historical film was planned, this material was rejected on visual grounds. That left Duradon. We accepted its drawbacks, which include a tendency to stretch over the course of time. We dismissed the health hazard argument (allergic reactions) in view of the small sail area involved. We used Dacron for the storm jib. This was cut from cloth weighing 340 grams per cm^2, to be on the safe side. All sails were made without battens as was customary with working sails in the early 1900s. The leech of the mainsail therefore had to be hollow which, unfortunately, reduced the efficiency of the sail. All the sails were made by the sailmaking firm of Segelwerkstatt Stade.

We opted for a Bermuda-style mizzen, as a gaff or lugsail would have been too large. Weather helm and difficult handling on a narrow, pointed stern would have resulted. The mizzen is well-suited as a steering sail and helpful when tacking because it can be pushed to windward using the boom. It also adds stability when lying to a sea anchor or a normal anchor. For this, it must be cut very flat. Only a single row of reef points is provided owing to the small area. The mizzen can be laced to the mast or secured with hoops.

The lugsail was selected for the main mast, as reported in Worsley's book. With a gaff-headed sail, the gaff would exert pressure on the mast and bend it. In addition, the lug rig requires only one halyard (instead of throat and peak halyards with a gaff rig). On the other hand, the gaff rig is more efficient when beating to weather. With a lugsail the yard need not be dipped (shifted). That makes for easier handling and tallies with Worsley's information. The yard is pitched at a steep angle, pushing the center of effort forward as much as possible and improving pointing ability. The jib can be cut larger, thereby reducing weather helm. The main yard is secured by a parrel, to hold the lugsail close to the mast when

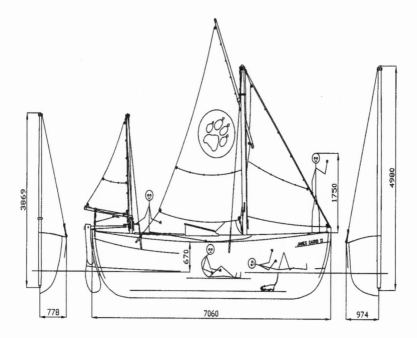

reefed. No boom is provided, something that is probably authentic. Actually, a boom would be advantageous as it makes handling easier and poles out the sail better when running before the wind, though a boathook can also do the job. The mainsheet of the lugsail is not led further aft for the following reasons:

> —less downdraft into the mizzen; important when close-hauled,
>
> —more room for the helmsman; and,
>
> —less weather helm.

When reefed, the lugsail also fits the mizzenmast; thus, in case of losing the mainmast, the mizzen can be moved forward to replace it.

The jib was cut as large as possible to reduce weather helm. This hampers forward visibility but, considering the amount of traffic that was to be expected, this was of little concern. For reasons already cited, the reefed jib would also fit the mizzenmast. The storm jib is even smaller than the reefed jib.

Arrangement of Shrouds and Stays

In the photos in Alexander's book *The Endurance*, the spreaderless shrouds of the JAMES CAIRD's masts run athwart the boat's centerline without crossing each other. No forestay can be seen on the 1916 mainmast; the jib was probably free floating; in this case our replica sacrificed authenticity for the sake of safety and ease of handling. The main shrouds were angled aft to counteract the pull of the headsail and to minimize sag in the jib luff. That's particularly important when sailing close-hauled. In addition, the jib hanks onto its stay, which greatly eases sail handling.

The shrouds of the mizzenmast are angled forward, thereby counteracting the pull of the mizzen. Since the double-ended JAMES CAIRD carries more beam forward, this also provides a better staying angle and enhances the stiffness of the rig. Similar arrangements are found in Colin Archer rescue vessels. In those boats, however, the forward rake of the shrouds is restricted by the turning radius of the main boom. It is unnecessary to have shrouds angled aft since the pull on the mizzen at the masthead is always aft and sideways.

Instead of modern turnbuckles, we use lanyards. They look authentic and are quite practical, as lanyards are easier to adjust than turnbuckles. It is important that the tensile strength of the lanyards match the tensile strength of the wire rope (a chain is only as strong as its weakest link). Shrouds and forestay are made of galvanized steel.

Masts and Spars

As was common practice in those days, the mizzen of the original was let into a notch in the thwarts so that it could be stepped easily. The mainmast of the JAMES CAIRD was stepped on the keel, which had to be reinforced just before leaving Elephant Island by bolting another lifeboat's mast alongside it. On the replica, both masts are stepped directly on a very solid keel of massive oak and held at deck level in their partners. Hence, they stood upright without stays. Masts and spars are made of thick Douglas fir. In case of a dismasting (a broken mainmast would be critical) the mizzenmast can be stepped in its place. It was possible to determine the length and position of the masts from the 1916 photos. The book *Bemastung und Takelung der Schiffe des 18. Jahrhunderts* was used a guide for the length of the lugsail yard. The length for the mizzen boom was determined arbitrarily.

Dimensioning of Masts and Standing Rigging

To determine the cross-sectional measurements for masts, spars and standing rigging, different and, at times, conflicting requirements had to be followed. First of all, the rig had to withstand all loads, i.e., without going over the side. The rigging had to be stiff—and not flex out of control—for the sails to hold their proper shape. Then the rig had to have the least possible windage to allow undisturbed air flow across the sails, which translated into better upwind performance.

The rig had to be light, to increase the righting moment. On the other hand, a heavier rig would increase the period of roll, which could help reduce seasickness for the crew.

At the beginning of the twentieth century, diameters for shrouds and stays—as well as masts and spars—were determined empirically. If something snapped or buckled, they made it thicker. If it didn't break, the measurements would be reduced—in part to save money. I get the feeling that this kind of thinking still persists today. Actually, precise calculation of rigging for sailing vessels is very difficult, even with today's computer technology.

This uncertainty starts with the load calculations. How big are the rig loads on various angles to the apparent wind, considering different sail combinations (some sails set or not set, reefed or unreefed), and the boat's motion in a seaway? Even if those loads were known in detail, there is still a three-dimensional, non-linear mechanical subsytem with loads in the standing rigging (great distortions, wires take up pull, but not pressure) and issues of stability (buckling of masts under pressure) that remains to be solved. Today, such a mechanical subsystem can be calculated on a PC, using the Finite Element Analysis (FEA).

At Kiel Technical College, we use computers to design rigs of modern yachts with many spreaders and stays; we also work out design loads for masts made of aluminum and carbon fiber. For the JAMES CAIRD II this method would be far too costly. Instead, a pragmatic three-step method was used.

For the first step, we used simple, empirical formulas taken from the book *Bemastung und Takelung der Schiffe des 18. Jahrhunderts.* The diameter of masts and spars can be determined, multiplying a factor by the respective length of the spar. We rounded up the numbers somewhat to allow for the rough seas of the Southern Ocean. Also, for lack of a formula, the mizzen boom length was simply eye-balled. We arrived at the following diameters: mainmast 12 cm; mizzenmast 8 cm; lug yard 7 cm; and mizzen boom 6 cm.

In the second step, we checked the values and calculated: (1) the tensile load of the standing rigging; (2) the maximum possible load on the rig; and (3) the maximum possible righting moment for the JAMES CAIRD II.

The maximum righting moment must balance with the heeling moment under wind pressure. For the most extreme case, we assumed that only the mainmast would carry sail and induce heeling moment. The righting moment (Mass x

Righting Arm) had to be estimated, because no calculations were available for it and the replica had yet to be built; otherwise, we could have measured the righting moment by running a heeling test. Mass was assumed to be three tons with the boat fully provisioned and a maximum lever arm at 0.33 meter. That results in a righting moment of one meter ton or ten kN. Dividing this value by the distance from the mast to the chainplate (approximately one meter) the pressure load for the main mast figures would be one ton or 10kN.

The mast is subjected to pressure. To calculate the dimensions, we can enlist Euler's buckling equation; using a safety factor of $v = 4$, the required moment of inertia of the mast "I" can be determined.

$$I = \frac{F \cdot L^2 \cdot v}{\alpha \cdot E \cdot \pi^2}$$

The unsupported length over which buckling occurs "L" is squared in the formula for the moment of inertia. Thus,

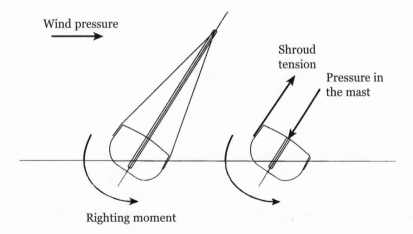

Wind pressure

Shroud tension

Pressure in the mast

Righting moment

short unsupported lengths yield small moments of inertia and, as a result, small mast diameters. For the mast of the JAMES CAIRD II the unsupported length is assumed to be the length between the deck and the hounds near the mast top "L" =3.7 meters.

As the mast is keel-stepped and held at deck level by the partners, i.e., firmly secured, the value = 2 is used for the fixed support. The modulus of elasticity for wood (Oregon spruce or Douglas fir) can be taken as E=10kN/mm². When we input the values mentioned, moment of inertia of "I"=277.4 cm⁴ results.

Then the minimum diameter of the mast can be determined from the moment of inertia "I."

$$D_{mim} = \sqrt[4]{\frac{64 \cdot I}{\pi}}$$

This gives a minimum mast diameter of Dmin = 8.67 cm. Thus, the mast diameter we found as 12 cm in the first step is on the safe side.

Shroud tension is determined in a manner similar to mast pressure load. The vertical component is the same size. To calculate the load on the shrouds, however, the vertical component must still be divided by the cosine of 12 degrees because the shrouds are set at an angle of about 12 degrees. We find a tensile load for the shrouds of 1.02 tons, or 10.22 kN—very similar to the pressure load which is one ton. Working out the minimum break strength of a shroud by multiplication with a safety factor of 3 for 3 tons requires galvanized steel wire with a diameter of 8 mm.

In the third step, the dimensions selected were checked

with the Nordic Boat Standard of Norske Veritas, which describes rigging designs for yachts up to 45 feet. The rules for rigging were programmed by a student, which made it easy to check the calculations quickly. It turned out that our dimensions were all on the safe side.

Although they appear oversized, the dimensions for the main mast from our calculations in step one were retained since the JAMES CAIRD II would be sailing the Southern Ocean. Without re-calculating the profile of the mizzen mast, we chose 8mm shrouds, the same diameter as those on the mainmast.

The first sea trials showed that the replica of the JAMES CAIRD has very little weather helm; that she is under-canvassed; that she can sail to weather even in strong winds though lacking a centerboard; and that she heaves-to very well under reefed jib and mizzen.

Professor Günter Grabe
Kiel Technical College, 1999

Bibliography

Alexander, Caroline. *The Endurance: Shackleton's Legendary Antarctic Expedition.* Frank Hurley, photographer. 1998

Carr, Tim and Pauline. *Antarctic Oasis: Under the Spell of South Georgia.* 1998

Heacox, Kim. *Shackleton: the Antarctic Challenge.* National Geographic

Huntford, Roland. *Shackleton.* 1986

Lansing, Alfred. *Endurance: Shackleton's Incredible Voyage.* 1984

McGregor Dunnett, Harding. *Shackleton's Boat: the Story of James Caird.* 1996

Mortimer, Gavin. *Shackleton und die Eroberung der Antarktis.* 2000

Reinke-Kunze, Christine. *Antarktis.* 1997

Shackleton, Sir Ernest. *South: the Story of Shackleton's Last Expedition 1914-1917.* 1991

Thomson, John. *Shackleton's Captain: a Biography of Frank Worsley.* 1998

Weyer, Helfried. *Antarctica.* 1998

Worsley, Frank Arthur. *Shackleton's Boat Journey.* Introduction by Edmund Hillary. 1998

Index